D1600185

MISSING
& PRESUMED
DEAD

About the Authors

Gale St. John was raised in a psychic family with her mother and maternal grandparents practicing psychic and spiritual beliefs. Gale has been a practicing psychic since she was a child. She's been teaching psychic development classes and conducting private psychic readings for over twenty years.

Gale is also certified in many areas of search and rescue work as well as having trained and certified with her dogs as a team for search and rescue. She spends much of her time working on missing persons cases and fulfilling the required training hours with her dogs. Gale is a member of a district task force for the disaster preparedness program, and is an emergency medical first responder in her state. While Gale holds many other titles, these are some of which she is most proud.

———

Diana Montane is a journalist and author. She began her career at the *Miami News*, and continued as entertainment editor of *EXITO*, a Spanish language weekly published by the *Chicago Tribune*.

Diana Montane co-authored *My Life as a Blonde*, the autobiography of talk-show host Cristina Saralequi, which was published by Warner Books; *The Daughters of Juarez* with Univision anchor Teresa Rodriguez, published by Simon & Schuster; *I Would Find a Girl Walking* with crime journalist Kathy Kelly, published by Penguin; and *Invisible Killer: The Monster Behind the Mask* with Sean Robbins, published by Titletown Publishing.

MISSING
& PRESUMED
DEAD

—————— A Psychic's Search for Justice ——————

GALE ST. JOHN
DIANA MONTANE

Llewellyn Publications
Woodbury, Minnesota

FIRST EDITION
First Printing, 2014

Cover design by Ellen Lawson
Cover images: iStockphoto.com/4801878/© Kristian Septimius Krogh
            iStockphoto.com/10431979/© atbaei
Editing by Connie Hill
Interior photos provided by the author

Llewellyn Publications is a registered trademark of Llewellyn Worldwide Ltd.

Library of Congress Cataloging-in-Publication Data
St. John, Gale, 1960–
  Missing & presumed dead : a psychic's search for justice / Gale St. John, Diana Montane.
     pages   cm
  ISBN 978-0-7387-3495-8
1. Parapsychology in criminal investigation—United States. 2. Parapsychology and crime—United States. 3. Missing persons—Investigation—United States. 4. Psychics—United States. 5. St. John, Gale, 1960– I. Montane, Diana II. Title. III. Title: Missing and presumed dead.
  BF1045.C7S7 2014
  133.9'1—dc23   2014011642

Llewellyn Worldwide does not participate in, endorse, or have any authority or responsibility concerning private business transactions between our authors and the public.

All mail addressed to the author is forwarded but the publisher cannot, unless specifically instructed by the author, give out an address or phone number.

Any Internet references contained in this work are current at publication time, but the publisher cannot guarantee that a specific location will continue to be maintained. Please refer to the publisher's website for links to authors' websites and other sources.

Llewellyn Publications
A Division of Llewellyn Worldwide Ltd.
2143 Wooddale Drive
Woodbury, MN 55125–2989
www.llewellyn.com

Printed in the United States of America

Dedications

Uncle Jim, this book is for you.—Gale St. John

For Mom, who believed in angels.—Diana Montane

Acknowledgments

I would like to thank my Aunt Marge and my Uncle Jim for encouraging me in my endeavors and giving me confidence in myself to carry them out. A big thank you to Jan for being a superior teacher and trainer, and in turn helping me set up great training standards for myself and my K9 kids. To my human kids, thank you for understanding my work and my times away from them. And last but not least, thank you, Rick, for years of believing in me and putting up with my need for space; for giving me the space.

—Gale St. John

Contents

FOREWORD

For me to be writing this foreword is the supreme irony. Why? The answer is simple: I'm the original "cop skeptic;" hardnosed, gotta see it to believe it, doubting Thomas. That is how my colleagues would describe me, and, if they are honest, how they would describe themselves as well.

Crimes are solved by clues, not visions. By cops, and not civilians. Ours is a world of shoe leather, phone books, and doorbells; not crystal balls, turbans, and astrology. That is what I used to think.

But life has a way of throwing you curve balls, and that's what happened when I first heard about Gale St. John. It was years ago and she probably never even knew it, but as a former detective and then lieutenant with the East Baton Rouge Sheriff's Office I like to keep abreast of law enforcement's latest and greatest.

Though Gale's name might not be as well-known as John Edwards or Sylvia Browne—at least not yet anyway—she has a stellar reputation in law enforcement circles and, unlike many other so-called "psychic detectives" who are often out for only themselves, Gale is what we cops call "the real deal."

We in law enforcement give such psychics a raw deal. I know. I've done it myself. Not only are we skeptics but we're often angry at the wasted time such people take away from "real evidence." And rightfully so; I've heard some of the craziest claims in the world from so-called psychics, and all they've gained us is wasted time and added frustration while real clues go unexplored and undiscovered.

But not Gale. I'd heard of her work on the Arizona case, even saw her profiled on Court TV, and since then have followed her career closely. She's not easy to find; not on the web, not on television, and not in the newspapers, but I think all that is about to change.

For her, I'm afraid, that will be a blessing and a curse. Even flying under the popular media's radar she's already overburdened with cases from as far away as California and Florida, Indiana and New Orleans.

I've never seen anyone work so tirelessly, and without compensation. The families don't pay her, the cops sure don't pay her, aside from maybe the occasional plane ticket and hotel room, and the media is twice as stingy. And yet she flies here and arrives there, meeting with cops who don't respect her and district attorneys who don't trust her, all because of the victim.

She's the ultimate volunteer, tromping up hills and down valleys, slipping on wet moss or freezing in deep snow, all to find a clue one of her spirit guides has shown her in the vast resources of her overworked mind.

She goes without sleep, food, and shelter—all to find a missing hotel room key, knives, guns, or, for that matter, any piece of evidence pertaining to a case. She sees things that would make cops blush, and has to deal with hundreds of family members' grief as she tells them the worst news they could ever hear.

And all without formal training. Cops? We get trained in everything: on the gun range, at the Academy, in the classroom. Gale was simply born with a gift that has caused her great joy and even more pain. What she's seen I can't imagine; what she's lived through few cops could bear. And still she soldiers on, with little compensation and even less recognition.

At last, I hope, Gale will get the respect she deserves. A former skeptic, now a true believer, I was not only proud to write this foreword but honored she would ask me.

On behalf of the victims, the families, and law enforcement everywhere, I would like to personally thank Gale for all she's done over the years. I know I'm supposed to be writing this, but I really think Larry King said it best when he interviewed Gale on his talk show recently.

Speaking to Raleigh Hendrickson, the father of a murder victim whose body—and her killer— Gale was eventually able to locate, Larry summed up what all cops feel, whether they care to admit it or not: "I'd take any avenue open to me ..."

Let's face it: When the clues have dwindled, the tip line's gone dry, the to-do list is done, the leads have dried up, and you know in your heart a killer's still walking the street, I'm with Larry: "I'd take any avenue open to me..."

For many of us, Gale has been that avenue. For you, now, she can be a gateway to a secret world, a world few of the more popular psychics would dare show you. Blessing? Curse? In her revelatory new book Gale reveals that her gift is a lot of both.

I hope you enjoy it...

—Lieutenant Karl Kretser (retired), author of *Danced to Death: The Desperate Hunt for a Serial Killer in Louisiana*

INTRODUCTION

Many people struggle to find their purpose in life, but I knew what I wanted to do from a very young age: help find missing persons. I didn't go the normal route that most may take and become a detective. I have been able to receive psychic messages and visions from a very young age, and thankfully I was raised in the Spiritualist religion, which encouraged me to embrace and use my abilities. When I first picked up on information in regard to the location of a missing local person and the body was located exactly where I pictured it, I knew I wanted to use my gifts to help others.

I don't work alone. I have trained dogs to recognize the decomposition scent of cadavers, and these dogs have been my coworkers and best friends. My daughter shares my psychic ability and started to accompany me on searches when she was eighteen. My granddaughter is also psychic and is following in her mother's footsteps.

This book will give you a glimpse into my life, a rundown of some of the cases I have conducted throughout the years, and how cadaver dogs are trained and used during a search for a missing person. My particular line of work is often criticized, but I will continue to do what I do for as long as I can because I've seen how what I find myself or lead others to find has helped families find closure and heal from the travesty of losing a loved one. Not every case is solved, but I will do whatever I can to help others find their loved ones.

Chapter 1

HOW I CAME TO BE

There have been endless debates about nature vs. nurture when discussing certain personality traits. In my case, I believe my gift was part of my nature, like some sort of gene or brain wave at birth. How I handled it as I grew up, however, was the product of nurturing. I was brought up in the Spiritualist religion. We believe in God, but also in spirits and the afterlife, which was the perfect atmosphere for me because I was able to see and communicate with spirits at a very young age. My gift was not ridiculed, so I didn't deal with a lot of the negative feedback many psychic children receive. We did what we call "billet readings" at our church where everyone in the congregation writes down a question, puts it in a box, passes it around, and the person doing the reading pulls one out. The reader holds the paper in his or her hand and answers that question. The answer, of course, comes from the world beyond. I started performing these as a young child and was absolutely certain of what those answers were. I could hear them.

When I was four years old, I was playing with the neighbor kids in our front yard, and my mom and grandma were around, but in and out of the house. I looked up and the neighbor's house was on fire. I was so scared I couldn't scream. I went and told my mother and my grandmother, and upon looking at the house, they told me that it was not on fire and that everything was fine. Four days later that same house caught on fire. My mom said, "Don't you dare say anything to anyone." If folks are skeptical about psychics now, you can imagine the way society was back in the 1950s and 1960s. I suppose my mom did not want me to be ostracized or labeled as weird or an outcast, but I was stubborn! Nobody should ever say "you can't" to me because I will go out of my way to prove them wrong. I said many things to people about their lives and private thoughts that were totally inappropriate, especially for a young child. I remember how obstinate I was and some of things I said to others and laugh about it to this day.

When I was younger, questions about the afterlife bothered me more than they do now. We Spiritualists believe in the permanence of the human spirit after death, and that those who have passed do speak to us. From the time I was five or six years old, we used to do what we called a circle. Almost my entire family consisted of psychics. Some were psychics, some were mediums, some were psychic mediums, and some were empaths. Those of us who were psychic would gather together on a regular basis. Everyone would sit in a circle, and we would all say a prayer and ask for protection. We'd use these circles to communicate with people who have passed away, most often family members. Sometimes people would sing to bring energy, and if there was someone guiding the circle as a trance medium, he or she would describe what he or she was seeing and hearing. Those that have passed on speak through the trance medium, utilizing the medium's vocal cords.

I had a teacher named Gertrude who was a Spiritualist minister and trance medium. She guided me on my psychic journey and she taught me to be a trance medium as well. I later would use trance mediumship to find missing people.

I had a major revelation when I was six years old. We were gathered together watching the local nightly news. Back in that day, everyone sat down together and watched news as a family. The news reporter relayed a story about a missing child, and I had a vision. I could see the little girl and knew her name and where she was. I knew the child wasn't injured or harmed in any way. I felt as though she was safe, although at the time I didn't understand parental abductions, which is what had happened in this instance. Apparently one parent had the girl and the other parent got in a panic and reported to the police that the daughter was missing, but I didn't feel the little girl was in any danger. I wondered if I would be able to find her. I blurted all of this information to my parents, who were a bit bewildered at what I had to say. It just came out of my mouth. It was something that was just inside me and I had to get it out. I told my parents that I wanted to help find missing people. I knew I could find them and help them, and I figured that I might as well help people out. This expression of goodwill and intention sounds great when you're seven, but you have no idea what else is ahead of you.

I started informally doing private readings to help find missing people when I was eleven. When I first started receiving information on missing person cases, I saw landmarks, and they are still what I first tune into to this day. I will see buildings and landmarks as if I was standing in front of the building itself. Messages such as distances and directions also come through as thoughts that pop into my head. The rumor mill was buzzing that I could help find missing people, and family members would come to our house and I would assist them in finding their missing loved one. I refer to the people I help as clients, even though I have never charged anyone money for information or for working on a case.

Chapter 2

THE BEGINNING

When I turned fourteen we moved out of the country and into the city. My parents and grandparents had owned the house for many years and rented it out before we eventually moved back.

I picked out the bedroom I wanted and was allowed to paint it the color of my choice: lilac. I loved my room and it became my sanctuary from all the family turmoil. My dad had lost his job, and he and Mom were trying to start a business selling ceramic molds and greenware. They went on the road a lot, so I was the one in charge of taking care of my grandmother, who lived with us and had a heart ailment.

As I lay on my bed one night, I began to see a boy in my visions. He seemed to be around my age. As I watched him more closely, I recognized his face. It was Kyle, who used to live in this house. His family had rented the house from my family for several years before we moved back in. I only saw

Kyle's face and remembered him as a daredevil and an adventurous kid, but in my vision he looked pale with eyes that seemed filled with questions and a deep sadness. I felt a bit confused by the difference between my knowledge of his personality and what I was seeing.

At the time I assumed I was seeing him because my room was the room he shared with brothers while the family lived in our house. I fell asleep after the visions evaporated. I didn't realize it at the time, but this was the beginning of my journey into the unknown and the unseen that would seal my fate.

It seemed as though I had only just closed my eyes when the alarm clock rang. I jumped up out of bed and began my morning routine to get ready for school. I was running late, so I grabbed my books and zipped out the door.

I had to walk one mile to school, and along the way I met a few of my friends. When we reached the half-mile point to our school, I saw my friend Jenny coming up to the corner, so I waited a minute for her to catch up.

As soon as she met up with me, Jenny said, "Did you hear about Kyle?"

I told her that I really did not know him well, other than when I saw him when we did repairs on our current house while his family was renting it.

Jenny got a strange look in her eyes and said, "Well, this is so scary! I just heard from Lisa. Her brother was good friends with Kyle, and Kyle's mom just called their house to find out if he had been there. Kyle was never there, and his mom is worried that maybe he ran away!"

I nodded, "Well, maybe he did, Jenny. A lot of kids do this around here."

We switched to another teen subject and marched into the school bus, which had just pulled up. Once inside the building, we split up and proceeded to our respective lockers, which were located on different floors.

While I was walking to my locker, I remembered Kyle's face so clearly from last night. I thought maybe it's just coincidence and went on with my school day. As the day progressed, I felt more and more bothered by the vision of Kyle's face, and felt an unsettling, uneasy feeling in the pit of my stomach.

I was reprimanded for not paying attention in my next few classes, so I was overjoyed when the last bell rang and school was over for the weekend. I was so happy about sleeping in the next morning and figured on spending a relaxing weekend with my friends and maybe going skating at the local rink on Saturday night.

When I got home, Grandma said that Mom and Dad were out in the garage, getting ceramic molds and greenware packed and ready to be delivered in the morning.

That evening I watched television till late. Around 1:00 a.m., I decided to head upstairs and go to bed. As soon as I crawled into bed, Kyle's face kept flashing before my eyes and through my half-closed lids. I thought this was crazy, I needed to get some sleep and I hadn't even thought about Kyle all night.

Then I started to hear a conversation. It was as if the group was not close enough for me to make out exactly what they were saying, but just close enough so I could hear the sounds of several people talking. I put my pillow over my head and tried my best to block out the noise and go to sleep, but the talking got louder and the voices got closer.

I said out loud, "I give up! What is it you want from me?"

Then I heard a new voice, different from the cacophony from before. It yelled: "LISTEN!"

I started to really focus on the voices since I was wide awake. I could hear several boys talking when all of a sudden one of them raised his voice and shouted angrily, "You got what you deserved the last time you screwed me over!"

I felt a great sense of dread and became very afraid. I then heard another voice say, "I ought to kill you for this!"

I tried with all my might to extricate myself from what was becoming a nightmare. I jumped out of bed, ran down the stairs, and turned on all the lights and the television to keep from seeing and hearing any of that awful conversation. My heart was pounding so hard I could hardly breathe. I could not wake Mom and Dad to tell them, and I wouldn't have dreamed of telling Grandma, as sick and frail as she was.

I took a blanket from the couch, wrapped it around myself, walked into the kitchen, and turned on the tea kettle. I thought a hot cup of tea would calm my nerves. After I fixed my tea, I went to the couch and sat in front of the television.

I sipped my tea and watched television for at least an hour, and the next thing I remember was Mom waking me up and saying, "Gale, what on earth are you doing down here?"

I said, "What time is it?" She told me it was 7:00 a.m., and that she and Dad were leaving in a few minutes. I was too afraid to tell her what I had seen and heard last night. After

Mom and Dad left, Grandma and I fixed breakfast. It tasted good, but I was not really into eating as tired as I felt.

Early that evening, Dad drove me to the skating rink where I met up with my friends. The place was so packed with kids we had a difficult time finding a place to sit to put on our skates. Once we had them on, we practically soared through the air and onto the ice. We were having a great time until they announced "boys skate only."

I motioned to my friends, pointing to the concession stand, that we should grab something to eat and drink.

As I bit into my slice of pizza, I heard Mary say the name I dreaded hearing: Kyle.

I nearly choked, then managed to say off-handedly, "Oh, did they find him yet?"

In a way, I did not want to know or even hear about this, but curiosity was gnawing at me inside. One of the other girls piped in, "No! And his mom is frantic! The police are questioning every one of his friends!"

I felt a panic inside and my breathing began to get more rapid. I wanted to blurt out what I had seen, but since moving to this new school, I had kept my abilities quiet and let no one know I was psychic. It was awful for me at my old school. Most of the kids made fun of me, and many of the parents of the kids who did want to be friends with me told them not to have anything to do with me. I didn't want this to happen again. Maybe I was just imagining the entire thing anyway.

Just then, the voice over the loud speaker said, "girls skate only." All of us screamed in unison, "Yeah, let's go!" I was happy and relieved, saved by the bell so to speak. I just wanted to enjoy the evening without having to hear the name Kyle again.

As I skated and tried to have fun, I was haunted by the voices I heard and what they said. I could not seem to shake off the fear inside me. I skated off the floor to a chair and sat there for a moment, trying to clear my head. As I sat there, I drifted into a vision. I saw the boys again and heard the voices. One was saying, "What's wrong with you, man? I did what you said." Then I saw them up in each other's faces. I felt so scared, as if I were there. I felt a touch on my hand and jumped up. It was Lisa. "What's wrong, Gale? Are you feeling okay?" she asked.

I told her, "Lisa, I am feeling a little sick. I will be okay in a few minutes." She told me, "Maybe you drank that pop too fast." I told her maybe she was right and left it at that.

I got up slowly and went back to skating. I stayed out on the ice for the rest of the evening, hoping not to see or hear anything else. It worked, but everyone kept asking why I was not taking a break to talk.

I felt so alone, even in the large crowd. I felt isolated and afraid, but of what? I had a confused and cluttered kind of feeling in my head and felt out of sync with the rest of the world. I'd had visions before, but nothing this disturbing. I just couldn't shake this awful feeling.

It was getting to be closing time, and I hurried to the pay phone to call Dad to remind him to pick me up. As I hung up the phone, Lisa came over to me and said, "Gale, all of us have been talking and we want to know why you are acting so strange. Are you mad at one of us? Did we say something to upset you?"

I said. "No, Lisa. I think maybe I am just tired because I did not get much sleep last night." This seemed to calm her down. "Oh, okay, well give me a call tomorrow and maybe we can all go to the mall to walk around for a while." I gathered up my skates and headed out the door to wait for my dad in the parking lot.

Dad was right on time, and when we got home, I went straight to bed. Much to my surprise, I woke up in the morning after a great night's sleep. I felt relief for the uneventful night and the dreamless sleep did wonders for me. I hoped I would not see any more visions or hear anything more about Kyle.

Feeling refreshed, I ran downstairs to ask Mom about going to the mall with my friends for a while. We all spoke on the phone and set up a time to meet. Mom dropped me off at the mall's theater entrance and the others were already there and waiting. We walked around, laughing and having a good time talking about school and other friends.

When it was time to leave, we all scattered and hurried out to meet our folks, and as I got in my mom's car, I realized that the day was going well and was uneventful as far as anything concerning Kyle. I felt happy and relaxed. Maybe it would all go away.

As soon as we got home, I rushed to my room to organize a report that was due at school the next day, and then do the dishes, which was my evening chore. I wanted to hurry and get things done so I could watch some television.

I sat down on the living room couch and turned on the television, but Dad said, "Let me watch the beginning of the news for a minute and then you can watch what you want."

I said, "Sure!" and I walked up and turned the channel to the local news station. I grabbed the comics section of the newspaper and figured I would read it while I waited for Dad to finish watching the news. As I sat down and began to read, I heard the name Kyle.

The anchor at the local news station was asking if anyone knew his whereabouts. They showed a picture of Kyle and told everyone to call the local police if anyone saw him. I felt that sinking feeling again, and wished I had not turned on the television.

Dad said, "Wow, I didn't know he was missing. Did you, Gale?" I said "Yes, I heard something about it at school, but everyone said he probably just ran away."

Dad listened to the rest of the news and then left the room. I quickly switched the channel to watch a movie that just started. I wanted this bad feeling to go way so I kept my mind on the movie.

After the movie ended, Mom came in and said, "Hey, you need to get ready for bed because you have school in the morning." I replied, "Yes, Mom, I know."

I walked upstairs slowly and took my time washing up and brushing my teeth, trying to put off going to bed. By now, I knew what would be waiting for me the minute I closed my eyes.

I crawled into bed with a complete feeling of exhaustion, as if I'd just run a marathon. This dreading what I might see was taking a toll on me. I finally fell asleep after a bit of worrying.

A noise woke me up around 4:00 a.m. I listened closely because I was not sure of what I had heard, but did not hear the noise again. I tried to get back to sleep, and while I was half in and out of sleep, I suddenly got sucked into another vision like a whirlwind. I was walking through an area that seemed familiar to me. I saw trees and tall brown grass, and then I spotted a body of water. I saw the sand and tree line and realized I was near the bay area.

I kept walking, and I felt as if I was really there. I could feel the sand under my feet and the grass touching my hands as I walked through it.

Oh no. No, I don't want to see this! I was scared as I turned and saw a large concrete drain pipe. It was very large in size, big enough for an adult human to crawl through.

I could not breathe and my stomach was in a knot as I looked to see what I really did not want to see. Yes, it's a body! I screamed at my vision and was so afraid. I could feel the killer there. He could see me too.

I was afraid for my life at this point. I tried to leave the area but I couldn't. It was keeping me there like a captive and there was no escape in sight.

I had to look at the body again. It was lying in a crumpled position. I could see it had been there long enough to start to decompose a bit and was a gruesome sight. The panic over-whelmed me and I tried to swallow with little success. Oh, God help me, it was Kyle.

As the worst of my fears swept over me like a cold wave, I felt the killer looking right through me. With all my might I pulled myself from the vision and gasped as I grabbed my pillow in horror. I knew where Kyle was, now what should I do?

I did not sleep the rest of the night, and in the morning I told my mom I was ill and needed to stay home. She placed her hand on my forehead and said, "You don't have a fever, but you do look very pale." She agreed I could stay home and I went to my room. I sat upright on my bed and tried to decide what to do. By the end of the day I decided that I must have imagined all of it and needed to forget it, but that vision haunted me.

I finally mustered up the courage and told Mom about my dream. I figured this would be the best and safest way to describe what I had seen. Mom brushed it off as the product of my overactive imagination and told me not to worry about such things. She said I may have had the dream because I saw the news story.

I had an uneventful night's sleep and went to school the next day, so I told myself Mom must have been right. But was she? I could not shake this sense of impending doom. There was a sense of finality, a tragic ending to what I felt, but I did not know what it was or what it meant.

Two weeks passed and I had no more visions, but I felt drawn to the bay area. I thought about having a friend drive me there, but the fear of what I saw and felt quickly overcame me. The fear of the killer still being close by and watching was enough to keep me from getting a ride to the bay.

I went to school on a Monday, two weeks after my last vision, and as soon as I got to school Jenny ran up to me and shouted, "They found Kyle!" She then said, in a very ominous tone, "It looks like murder." I asked, "Where?" and she said, "I have no clue yet. This is all I heard from another friend."

The day seemed to drag on and I was tempted to call my parents and tell them I was sick and needed to come home, but I knew they were busy getting ready for another road trip. I had a lot of time to think during the one-mile walk back home from school, but my mind was racing all over the place.

When I walked in the door, I half expected Mom and Dad to say they'd heard about Kyle, but they were too busy to have even taken the time to turn on the morning news. As 6:00 p.m. rolled in, I darted to the television as fast as I could to see if there was any news about Kyle. Dad came into the room to take a short break. He said he wanted to catch the weather report before leaving.

I listened to all the local news and at the end they said, "Stay tuned for an update on the earlier story of a body found in the bay area." I choked and swallowed hard. I knew it was Kyle. It seemed as if an eternity passed as the commercials came on and then ended. I counted four of them. My heart was pounding as the news came back on. The reporter said, "Here is an update on the body found in the bay area. The body found in the bay area has been determined to be that of a missing youth named Kyle. Authorities suspect foul play, so if you have any information, call the local police."

That's it, that's all they said. Dad yelled out to Mom, "Hey Irene, did you hear about the kid who used to live here?" She said, "Yes, I could hear. I can't believe it!"

I protested, "But Mom, I told you I had a dream about this and that is where I saw him!" She said, "Yes, Gale, but who would you have told? What would happen if you told? Do you understand that if you say these sorts of things you could be a suspect and even tried for murder?" I never thought about that. I realized this was true and something I needed to figure out. But I did know where his body was, and I also knew the killer's face.

This episode marked the end of my childhood dreams. I saw Kyle's body and was taken there as if I was living it myself. I couldn't even scream. I was walking and I felt the killer's eyes on me in a dreamlike state, but it was a lucid dream. I did not like the feelings I had or things I saw, so I did everything I could to ignore my ability for almost two years. I didn't want to do anything with it, nor did I ever want to see anything like I did with Kyle, but the more I tried to avoid my abilities, the more it kept going.

My experience with Kyle's disappearance and murder changed me forever and set my life on a collision course with all the skeptics of the world. It was not a path I might have chosen if I had been at a different stage in my life. Or did this path just choose me and I really had no capabilities to stop this gift of second sight from the angels?

Chapter 3

A WAKEUP CALL

I got married when I was sixteen, and we had some paranormal phenomena happen in our house. It was sort of my own version of *The Exorcist*. Things flew off the dressers. It was an experience that really woke me up. My husband did not believe any of the psychic stuff and we never talked about it. I went to see the film like everybody else and laughed at it like everybody else.

Shortly after I had seen the movie, I was in a really bad car accident. I was lying in bed, trying to sleep, but I was in excruciating pain. I was also experiencing emotional pain since one of our cats was dying despite our desperate attempts to save its life. Suddenly, the bedroom door, which was on my husband's side of the bed, slammed shut. He had been sleeping, but bolted up, yelling "What the hell is going on?" and the whole room turned dark. Mind you, at that point I'm also wondering what the hell is going on. Then I felt hands on my neck and thought it was my husband. I then saw him on the other side of the bed and he was screaming. I didn't feel like I was being choked but I felt hands on my neck. I then saw pictures in front of the windows. We were in a second- floor apartment so I knew it wasn't something outside on the street. At this point I was saying to myself, "Okay Gale, don't panic." Things were flying off the dressers, I was laughing, and my husband was screaming. All of a sudden I hit the wall and the hands were really choking me. The room was filled with figures in hoods and were chanting in unison. I thought, "Oh my God, they are really going to kill me!" I was so scared. I thought about my grandfather, who had recently passed away. My husband was trying to get the door to open but could not get it to budge. I hollered, "Grandpa! Help!" The door flew open and the handle punched a hole in the wall. The room was flooded in a very bright light that blinded me. As suddenly as it appeared, it was gone. I could hear my grandfather say, "Turn on all the televisions and radios in the house!" We went out in the living room and found that the cat had died.

I later learned that the woman who lived there before we did was involved in black magic. She would conduct rituals and hold gatherings at the apartment, and it was apparent that negative energies and entities were still in the apartment. The dying cat most likely attracted those forces. I never watched *The Exorcist* again, and it was at this point I realized that there was evil in this world, and we had to have balance. Things became a little more clear and began to make sense, and maybe that part of me matured.

It was shortly after this experience that I decided this would be my life's mission. It was kind of like saying, you have to choose sides. There is no middle. You're good or you're bad. I could sit idly by and ignore the things I saw, or I could put them to use.

Chapter 4

TAKING MY ABILITIES AND RESPONSIBILITIES SERIOUSLY

I was eighteen when I worked on my first official case. I gave unsolicited information to a family as to where a missing person could be found and that the person was not dead. I was twenty-one when I was approached by a man who asked me to assist him in finding his wife who was missing and presumed dead.

I saw something that said twenty-one, and I didn't know if it was a highway. I could see sixteen miles west. The client said, "Okay, that sounds familiar." Then I said, "I keep seeing a church, and the funny thing about this church is I see a picket fence that goes across the front but it doesn't fence anything in. When I look catty corner across from the church I see horse fencing. But just before that it looks like some kind of creek, a short underpass, and then really tall fencing with a pump or something, and it's something having to do with her being there." My client drove around an area that he knew looked like the one I described and called the police. The cops walked around the area and found one of the woman's shoes, which the husband verified as his wife's. At that point the police sent the husband home, and they located the body four or five hours later. She had been buried in a shallow grave around five or six more miles down the road. If the police hadn't found her shoe, they would not have continued to look for her body. This was the first time the police were able to find the missing body through information I had passed along to my client.

Word spread slowly about me after that, but it was so taboo back in the 1970s and 1980s. Once every six months or so, someone would ask me to help. The cases would appear on the news, but the families never talked to me or mentioned to the police how they obtained the information where the person was located because there was still that stigma attached to what I do. It was very thankless but it didn't stop me from doing it.

I came to a point where I would go out and search for a person if he or she had gone missing near my house without hearing from the family. In 2001 I decided I needed a dog to continue my searches. Some missing people are buried, and I can't dig up a one-mile by one-mile area in order to find their body, but a dog that is trained to find cadavers can pinpoint where a body is buried. If I approach the police with a general location, they won't bring their dogs out because it costs money. I figured if I got a dog, I would be able to provide a more specific location to speed up the recovery process, but I knew I had a long road of dog training ahead of me.

Chapter 5

"MY ROOMMATE! MY ROOMMATE!"

I have had encounters with the dimension where souls live when they have not yet crossed over to the other side, but my first bona fide experience that dealt with a missing person's case occurred in 1992.

My reputation had spread throughout the Midwest area, and in August 1992, I received a phone call at my home in Toledo, Ohio. The man on the other end of the line seemed nervous. He said his name was Raleigh and he needed to talk to me. He asked if he could come to my house to discuss his missing daughter, Stacy, who had been living in Tempe, Arizona, while attending a local university.

In a calm, but somewhat reluctant voice, I said, "Sure." The reason I hesitated was that I was pregnant with my youngest child, Dustin, who was due any day. I was feeling so tired and unsure of my strength I did not know if I was up to the task.

The next morning there was a knock at my door. It was Raleigh. He was shaking and seemed unsure of why he was coming to me. He sat down in one of the armchairs in my living room and began to fidget. He had brought a picture of his daughter, and when I reached across the table to take the picture from him, our hands touched.

I saw his daughter, Stacy, right away. I held the picture in one hand and began asking him questions. I asked him for the color of her hair and her date of birth. I suppose I did this just to buy myself some time as I tried to figure out how to tell him that Stacy was standing next to me and talking, and this meant she had already passed to the other side.

In the picture her dad had shown me, she had light brown hair and a beautiful smile, but the face I was seeing in my vision was quite different. Her hair and eye color were the same, but her facial expression was quite different. She had a look of utter desperation, and her face was tense with anxiety.

Finally, I drew a deep breath, grabbed Raleigh's hand and said, "I am sorry to tell you this, but Stacy has passed. She is no longer with us. But she is here, right next to me, telling me what happened."

Raleigh broke down in tears. When he regained his composure, he said, a bit more steadily, "I need to know what happened to her and where she is." I told him a few bits and pieces of what I was seeing, but held back on some of the information. I do that in order not to cloud my judgment with extraneous information a family member might offer.

Raleigh asked me if I was willing to talk to the detective assigned to the case. I agreed and told him that if the detective was willing to talk, so was I.

I received a call from the detective the next day. He told me that he was with the Arizona Police Department and that Raleigh had asked him to contact me in regard to Stacy's case.

I told the detective everything I learned about Stacy, what happened to her, and where it took place. The detective said Stacy's father told him I said Stacy had passed, and asked me how I would know this. I told him straight out that Stacy was talking to me, and the only way she could be talking to me was if she was no longer alive.

At that point, the detective seemed to take offense that I was telling him his missing person was dead. I could tell by the sudden change of tone in his voice. He then started to ask me questions but I could sense he was extremely skeptical about psychics, which have gained an unfair and even laughable reputation with law-enforcement agencies. However, as we talked, the room where I was sitting in my house began to fade. I knew what I now could see was the crime scene and Stacy's final resting place.

I told the detective what I had experienced and he asked me to describe what I could see around me. I felt as though I was really walking through the area. I looked down and saw cracked dirt that gave the appearance of giant puzzle pieces. I glanced up and saw large earthmoving equipment. He asked me if I saw anything else in the area, and I said, "Yes, I see palm trees."

In my vision, I walked a little farther and came upon a fence and a building. As I relayed this to the detective, he asked me to describe the scene. I said the building appeared to be built of corrugated metal, with one door and a window that seemed to be made of the same metal. I looked around and saw water and a large pile of dirt. All of a sudden I seemed to zoom right through the pile of dirt and saw Stacy in the water. I felt a terrible sharp pain in the back of my head. It was then that I realized Stacy had been shot in the back of her head. I also felt both of my wrists hurting, as if my hands had been tied behind my back.

I told the detective all of this and he said, "Are you sure?" Once again I could feel the detective's tone of voice turn more abrupt, as if I were disrespecting him in some way. He stated in a very curt voice that he had written it all down and if he needed more information he would call me. I could tell he only called me in order to satisfy the father's request, so I just let it go and said, "That's fine, detective. Call me if you need to." We hung up, but I knew he would call again once he realized I knew what I was talking about.

Two days later, I received a phone call from the detective. He told me they found Stacy, and when he went to the scene it was exactly as I described it. He then admitted with a slight laugh that initially he tucked my number and description of the site away in a file and figured that he was done with me. I am more than used to encountering this attitude, mostly from the police, but from some families as well. Once they find out how on target I am with the information I provide, then they want more. And sure enough, the detective wanted more information, knowing he had a killer on the loose.

I described a man to him and gave him just a short and to-the-point description of a man I saw in a vision, as the officer was in a hurry. Two days went by and the detective called me. He said, "Gale, I think we have the guy." Just as the detective was giving me the lowdown on his suspect, I saw Stacy Hendrickson again. She was very insistent, raised her voice, and kept repeating, "My roommate!" She proceeded to show me the crime scene, and then I understood what she was trying to get across to me: her roommate was in danger! I immediately relayed this information to the detective. I told the detective that Stacy's roommate would be killed by the same man who killed Stacy. He said, "It's not going to happen because we have him." I said, "No, you do not! Stacy says he is a local man who works at a fast food restaurant in the area, and that he and the roommate are dating, or he feels he is dating her."

I told the detective that the roommate knew this man and planned to go out with him that very evening, and he must act quickly in order to stop this murder. I also warned that this guy would seem very cool, calm, and collected, but to not be fooled by this. I said, "This man is going to try to hurt you. Be careful."

Later that day, Raleigh called me to tell me investigators had located Stacy's body. I told him what the detective had called to tell me, but as I spoke to Stacy's father I saw another body. I told Raleigh he needed to tell the detective to drive about thirty miles west from his office to a place that most people considered a bad area or a dumping ground of sorts. I felt the detective would know the site. It had a bit of a musty smell with tar mixed into it.

I saw a girl around nineteen years old, with dark brown hair. I could see her body was about thirty to fifty feet off the road. I told Raleigh, "Tell the detective that this is not tied to Stacy's case." Raleigh told me he was calling the detective and then leaving from Toledo, Ohio, for Tempe, Arizona, the next morning.

The detective called me the next morning. He said he picked up Stacy's roommate's "friend," and when he brought him in for questioning, he was indeed cool, calm, and collected. He did admit to doing the crime but said it was an accident. The detective said he confronted the man with the fact this accident scenario was not consistent with the shooting. And then without warning, the suspect threw a punch at the detective, who thankfully had the forewarning and ducked, and the suspect smashed his fist right through the plaster of the wall in the interrogation room. The detective said, "Hey, thanks for the warning!" and laughed. What I did not tell the detective was that while I was speaking with him early that morning, I was already in labor with my youngest son, Dustin, and headed for the hospital as soon as I got off the phone.

When I came home from the hospital two days later, I had a message from Raleigh on my answering machine. He said, "Gale, I just wanted to tell you that the detective did find the other body the day I told him to look."

That is another story, and I do not know the outcome of that case. All I know is that the other girl came to me and wanted to be found, and with Stacy's help, she was. Stacy's roommate was safe.

The suspect who was seeing Stacy's roommate admitted he broke into the apartment late one night. When Stacy woke up, she became angry, so he tied her up and shot her to death.

On December 3, 2004, I appeared on *Larry King Live* to talk about Stacy's case. King introduced me as "the only psychic who has prevented a murder." Raleigh was also on the show, and he and I talked about the entire case. As King was about to sign off, Raleigh jumped in, "I'd like to say something, Larry." King said, "Yeah, quickly, Raleigh."

The father spoke somewhat hurriedly given the time allowed, but he had his say:

"I think police departments around the country should listen to these psychic people. I think they don't want to—it's like hocus pocus to them. But I think they should treat it, if they find the person credible, I think they should use it as a credible lead and follow up on it because I think it can—lives can be saved. And after all, the main thing is to find the perpetrator and get him off the street. And I think…"

Time was really running out, but King wrapped it up by saying, "I'd take any avenue open to me."

Chapter 6

IF I HAD GONE

I don't have to be at a location in order to have a vision or receive information as to where to find the missing person. I can pass along information to others at the location, who can go and investigate, as I did with Stacy's case. I was unable to go to that case due to family obligations, but a case I was involved with in the mid-1990s made me realize how effective I could be if I was on location.

In 1994, I received a call about a missing man from the Roswell, New Mexico, area. The very soft-spoken man on the other end of the phone line began to tell me the story of his missing son, Stephen.

As we spoke, I began to see a vision and hear words that made little to no sense to me, but I told the father anyway. I saw tall pine trees and received the impression that this also had something to do with the name of a place. I saw a campsite not too far from the area and a pickup truck. I felt that the truck was Stephen's, and his father confirmed that the truck had been found. I heard the word "captain," but only knew that this was the name of an area, so I told Stephen's father what I'd heard. I described the vastly dense area full of small cliffs and rocky, rugged terrain. I told him that Stephen would be found near a place with the name of "captain." He told me he thought he knew of this place.

I told the father that I felt that his son had passed and that a bear had been the culprit and not foul play.

I also felt that he might not be found for a long time due to the terrain. Of course, the father was not happy to hear this, and it was the last time I ever spoke to him.

Stephen was found in 2004 in the exact place I indicated.

In May 2004, Bob, a member of our search and rescue team, sent me this email from the New Mexico Search and Rescue Team:

"Hikers found skeletal remains among rugged terrain near Capitan Peak, and positive identification was made this month using dental records from the U.S. Army. This brings closure to a case pending since May, 1993. A search lasting a total of six days was conducted in the Pine Lodge area, on the east end of Capitan Mountain, using well over a hundred searchers from numerous volunteer teams, the U.S. Border Patrol, and the airmen from the Roving Sands Exercise being held in southern New Mexico at the time. The search was initiated after Stephen's pickup was found near a campsite. No trace of Stephen was found at that time."

The case of Stephen Summerville is one of the cases that prompted me to go out to the locations and do the searches myself. If I could have gone to New Mexico, I am certain that I would have located him.

Chapter 7

JIMMY, KING OF THE ONE-WORD CLUES

I received a flood of calls after my appearance on Larry King's show in 2005. Some calls were from nut cases and some were more serious in nature. Approximately two weeks after the show aired, Raleigh, whom I had worked with on his daughter Stacy's case, was at a karaoke bar he often frequents.

A young woman came into the bar and asked the owner if she could post a flyer about her missing brother, whose name was Jimmy Caine. The owner said she could, and as Raleigh walked up to look at it, the girl posting the flyer recognized him. She introduced herself as Linda, and said, "Hey, aren't you the man I saw on *Larry King Live*?" Raleigh acknowledged that yes, he was. Then she asked him, "Do you know how I can get hold of Gale St. John?" He replied, "Yes I do, but I sort of screen the people I send to her."

Linda told Raleigh about her brother and why she needed to contact me. He gave her my number and told her, "If anyone can help you, it is Gale."

The next day I received a call from Linda. I was a bit leery since I had been getting a lot of calls from people out in left field, wanting to know about aliens and such. When she explained she'd gotten my number from Raleigh I felt better, but I was still somewhat apprehensive. Nonetheless, I agreed to meet with several family members at the motel where the brother was last seen on November 24, 2004.

It was the week before Christmas and we had been lucky so far with the weather with small flurries of snow here and there, although the temperatures were bitterly cold.

My daughter Tamra was eighteen at the time and went with me on this expedition for the first time. She shares my psychic abilities, and after years of hearing me talking about cases, she wanted to participate and help me with my life's work. She now goes with me on most of my cases and has been a fabulous asset to me, as well as the families we work with. Tamra is also my protector and takes notes when she's on an investigation with me. When I am seeing something, I am not aware what is going on around me. My sole focus is on what visions are unfolding before me, so Tamra is there to make sure I stay safe and take notes of what I'm relaying to her as to what I'm seeing.

Tamra and I left for the motel about an hour early, so I would have plenty of time to find it and then go get coffee while we waited for the family to get there. Well, the coffee never happened. When I got to the motel and pulled into the parking lot, I began seeing things right away. The visions were very clear, and it was like I was seeing everything unfold right in front of me. These visions are so clear, it is like watching television. If I get these when I am driving, I do try to pull over when it happens, but sometimes it happens faster than I can find a safe place to pull over. I also felt deep anger. I saw a man who wasn't Jimmy, and then I felt as though I needed to leave that motel and that I would see more of what happened if I got in the car and started driving, though at this point I had no idea where I was being led.

I turned out of the parking lot and drove about four miles, crossing the border into Michigan. I was led to another motel. I pulled into the parking lot and felt a fight was going to happen. I saw a man and a woman get into a car along with Jimmy. I saw the car go down one block, stop, and the men got out. A fistfight ensued. Then they got back in the car and I knew they went to buy drugs at a crack house in North Toledo.

As I sat there, I realized it was time for me to meet Linda, her sister Karen, and Jimmy's wife at the motel. I drove the four miles back to the original motel, and within a few minutes they all showed up. It was very cold, so I called them all in to sit inside my van so we could talk and I could relay what visions I had just seen in regard to Jimmy.

Linda started off by giving me a recap of Jimmy's last whereabouts, and a flood of new information came to me. I told them what I'd seen before I met up with them, but then I focused on what I was currently witnessing.

I started seeing a house with almost no paint. It was very run down with a porch with missing boards and in such bad condition it was no longer of any use. I saw that the house had an alley next to it and one behind it. The front door looked as if it had been broken into. As I walked around to the back of the house in my vision, I saw a wrought iron rail on the ground and one still connected to the three rickety back steps. The rails were covered with rust.

I was describing this to the three family members, and everyone was silent. I thought I said something wrong, but Linda said, "Could I call my brother Sam and have him come here to hear this?" I said it was fine. Linda said she could not believe the accuracy in my description of the crack house, which was located in North Toledo. She and Sam had gone there looking for Jimmy after he disappeared.

Sam soon arrived and jumped in the van with the rest of us. I then received more information. I described a man I saw, which fit the description of a relative of Jimmy's. I knew this man knew what happened to Jimmy, or at least had a very good clue of what went down. I saw a drug deal happen and money was exchanged. Someone was ripped off, there was another fight, and the two men parted ways. The relative walked away and Jimmy drove back to the hotel.

At this point, Linda asked the question I had been dreading, "Is Jimmy alive?"

How do you say this tactfully? No matter what you say or how you say it, the facts are still the facts. I drew in a deep breath and said calmly, "I am so sorry, but he is right here with me. He is dead." The tears flowed down their faces as they tried to stay composed. Linda then said, as she wiped away the tears, "Now what? Where is Jimmy?"

I was seeing a few clues such as a creek and concrete over water. I asked if they checked the area next to the motel. They told me yes and even the police checked that area and didn't find anything. Well, that seemed to rule out that location. I didn't have any other information to relay, but I told the family I would let them know if I received any more in regard to Jimmy's disappearance.

The first time I saw Jimmy he was in a fetal position and refusing to talk to me. I understood why after his sister, Lisa, told me that Jimmy did not believe in the afterlife. I had not heard a word from Jimmy until the middle of January. I was driving Tamra and myself to the store across town, and just as I got off the expressway, I heard Jimmy's voice. He said "KEY" loud and clear. Jimmy was finally ready to start talking. He and I immediately hit it off in a way I understood. He had a wonderful sense of humor, loved to joke around, and was starting to deal with his untimely death. He now was able to show me a picture and give me impressions.

Needless to say, I never made it to the store. Jimmy directed us to a vacant store next to the Ohio/Michigan border, which was not far from the hotels where Jimmy and the other men would meet up.

When we got out of the car, the temperature was freezing and the wind was almost sweeping us off our feet. The wind chill felt like sharp needles on my face and my fingers were near frozen, despite my mittens, after twenty minutes of walking and searching.

My daughter, who had been complaining the entire time because she had her heart set on going to the store, said,

"Mom, listen. I am freezing, this is stupid, and we're never going to find a key in the snow, in this wind."

I said, "Yes, we are. Jimmy says we are."

Tamra then asked what the key looked like. I told her Jimmy showed me a key with a plastic piece on it. Tamra said, "Yeah, right, Mom, and we are going to die out here looking for a needle in haystack."

Just as she was done complaining, she yelled, "Mom, quick, get over here!"

I ran to see what it was, and there it was, the key, gleaming in the sun, with the plastic key chain right out in plain sight as Jimmy showed me it would be. The snowplows must have scooped it up and pushed it to the surface. I picked it up with a tissue and dropped it into a plastic bag I had in my car.

I looked at the key as I tried to get warm, and saw the number ten on the plastic key chain. I drove to the only two motels just over the state border. One motel did not have a room ten, and it was not the motel I saw where the fight took place. I drove to the other motel, went to number ten, and saw that the door was kicked in.

I asked one of the people who lived there, and he said the door was broken around the last week of November and had not been fixed since. I grabbed my cell phone and took a picture just in case I needed it. To me this proved what Jimmy said, that he had been in a fight here, and this was part of what took place before his death. I called Linda and relayed to her what I had found and told her I would let her know if anything more came to me.

Two weeks later Jimmy's wife called to see if I had I had no more information, but I hadn't been able to make a connection with Jimmy since I had received the word "KEY." I thought that if I got together with the family, I'd be able to more freely communicate with Jimmy. We all gathered at Linda's house and I gave her the key that Tamra found. I began with leading everyone in a prayer and I focused on Jimmy and hoped that he'd provide some information. I heard a name, which didn't make any sense to me, but the family said it was the name of a local drug dealer. I also heard the words "pressed" and "sealed." I had no idea what they meant, and neither did anyone else. Nothing else came through and I ended the session feeling very disappointed. Cases can be very difficult at times, but I was getting very frustrated. These one-word clues that were coming forward were not very helpful and I frankly didn't know what to do. I did blurt out a prediction to Jimmy's distraught family that I felt he would be found in mid-April. I tend to blurt things out like this without thinking, and thankfully in previous cases they have happened. I was hoping something would happen in the next few months so that what I said was true.

On April 17, I felt a need to drive to where I found the key. When I got there, I looked around and felt nothing except pure frustration. I looked up and yelled out loud, "Jimmy, talk to me!" and just as soon as I said it, Jimmy yelled back at me, "Spicer!" I laughed and said, "Sure, Jimmy, give me more I can't understand! You are the king of one-word clues!"

It was getting dark so I decided to go home and see what I could find out on the Internet. I felt that Spicer must be a street name, and when I put it in the map search engine, it said there was no such street name in Toledo. I was frustrated and decided to go to bed.

The next morning I was still bothered by the Spicer clue so I called my oldest daughter, Diana, who is a nurse. I asked her if she ever heard of a street named Spicer and why I was searching for a street with that name. I told her that my Internet search said there wasn't a street named Spicer in Toledo, but that I couldn't shake the feeling the name was dealing with a street. Diana said she didn't know of a street with that name but that she had a Toledo street guide and would look it up once she got off of work.

That afternoon, Tamra and I went to a store in West Toledo that was not far from where I first met with Jimmy's family. I kept having recurring feelings of urgency, almost like anxiety attacks, when I was at the store. Diana called me on my cell phone when I was on the store and said, "Mom, I looked up the street name and found it. It is a real street." And then she said, "Mom, I feel this is urgent and you need to go now." I told her I was feeling the same thing and knew that we had to immediately go to Spicer Street. Tamra and I left our shopping cart in an aisle and ran out of the store, leaving a wake of strange looks from the customers and employees of the store. Tamra and I hopped in the car and drove away while Diana gave us instructions as to how to get there.

As I wound through a small neighborhood, I came to a street with the name Spicer. It was a short street—only a few houses long. As I sat there looking down the street, I saw an open lot between two houses. I pulled the car up to the empty lot and stopped to look.

As I sat there I said to Tamra, "I don't get it." But as soon as I said it, I looked straight in front of me and I realized I was could see the buildings on the next road over from Spicer. I was looking directly at the motel where I first met Jimmy's family. I could even see the motel sign from the empty lot. It seemed as though this empty lot between the two houses was forming a picture that was indicating to me to focus on the next street.

I looked to my left and saw the edge of a building that housed a window manufacturing company that also made seamless siding and gutters. Just as I started to figure things out, I heard Jimmy say, "Pressed and sealed." I threw my car in gear and floored it because I had finally realized where Jimmy's body was. I pulled into the window company parking lot and jumped out of my car with Tamra running behind me. I felt like a hound dog on a scent. I could not stop myself until I was in back of the building and was walking next to the creek as fast I could. The feeling got stronger and stronger as I inched toward the road, which was a somewhat main thoroughfare and had a fair amount of traffic. I said, "I have to go across the street." Tamra pulled me back onto the sidewalk, held onto me until it was safe to cross and then released me. I was operating as if I was on autopilot. I would have walked right into traffic if she wasn't there, so I greatly rely on her to help keep me safe when I'm on a mission.

As I crossed the road, I first stayed on the right side of the creek, then after about five feet, I said, "No, I need to be on the other side." We quickly made it to the other side and Tamra said, "I'll go down the steep bank while you stay up here." I had recently suffered a hip injury and realized it wasn't the best thing for me to be crawling down there.

I started to slow down and became calmer. The extreme sense of urgency was lessening, so I knew we were very close to discovering something. I had walked for about fifty feet when I heard my father, who had passed away several years ago. He yelled, "CALL HER UP NOW!"

At first I did not understand this, and then suddenly the words came out of nowhere. I yelled in a panicked voice, "Tamra, come here now!" She ran up the bank toward me, and I took about five or six steps and felt a hand on my shoulder. I thought it was Tamra's hand, but as I looked back, I saw her about five steps back. Then I heard a voice say, "Turn and look down." It was Jimmy's voice. I realized it was his hand I felt on my shoulder. I felt my heart lurch into my throat as I turned to look down the bank. Jimmy said, "Turn and look. That's me."

I looked down into the creek. Jimmy's lifeless body was about twenty feet from a small cement bridge over the creek. I walked to the bridge with Tamra and tried to remain calm as I called Linda and Karen, but my hands were shaking and dialing was difficult. I told them to get the family over here right away.

I sat in the grass with Tamra and we shed a few tears and said a prayer together. Jimmy's entire family showed up about ten minutes later. Linda, Karen, and Sam climbed down the bank to identify the body. Linda was crying and somewhat hysterical but managed to say, "Yes, it is Jimmy! I saw the tattoo of his kids that he had on his back." The family then called the police.

The date was April 17. Just as I had predicted, we'd found Jimmy's body by mid-April.

The day after I found Jimmy, he came back to me and impressed me with the feeling that his family needed to go back to where his body was found. I called them and they met me at the site.

Once everyone was back where Jimmy's body was discovered, Linda asked me, "What is it?" I told them that Jimmy told me there were items that belonged to him that were at the site. Karen said, "But the police said they did a clean sweep of the area." I insisted, "Jimmy says no!" Karen crawled across the small stones and made her way under the bridge. Much to everyone's surprise, she found his car keys.

Jimmy's family still had questions about what happened between the time he was last seen and when his body was discovered. The local news outlets and police departments were asking anyone who had any information in regard to this case to come forward. The area had been searched two weeks prior to finding Jimmy's body and no clues were unearthed then. The body was not at the creek at that time.

A local man contacted the police and stated his two sons had been at the exact spot by the creek a day before Jimmy's body was discovered and they hadn't seen anything. But dead people do not just get up and walk. How did Jimmy get there that day? Locals had reported seeing a car that drove into the grassy area near the creek the night before the body was discovered, but nothing concrete came from that lead.

When the coroner's office performed the autopsy on the body, they found he had ingested a lot of Tylenol and there was a plastic, tubular implement connected to his mouth. His two front teeth were found in the back of his throat. Jimmy's death was ruled a suicide, but I still have many unanswered questions. I'm just glad that I was able to find him and have his family gain some closure.

Jimmy now helps me with some of my cases. I suppose he was pleased with the outcome of his own case, and wants to seek justice for others; a justice he did not receive. The first sign I get from Jimmy is his laugh, his infamous impish laugh.

I was particularly frustrated during another case, and in what has now become a habit with us, I said, "Jimmy, where are you when I need you?" I heard his laugh and said, "Really, Jimmy? Really? I need help here, and you're leaving me hanging? I'm heading to Florida. Put your hand in this because I need to be guided to the right place." I could feel his presence. I said, "Jimmy, are you there! This is the moment." He started to laugh. No words were needed.

Chapter 8

THE HARTMAN KIDS

I receive a number of phone calls from people who live in the same region as I do because of word of mouth and due to coverage on some of the cases in which I've been involved. I received a phone call on May 30, 2005, from Jean, an elderly woman who lived nearby. After talking to her on the phone, I agreed to meet with her, and drove to the area where she lived to hear more about what she had to say. I don't know why I felt like this case was something I had to do, but I felt I had to appease this older woman.

I met Jean at her house and she instructed that I follow her to the place where she wanted me to get a sense of what might have happened. She led me to an old farm near her house and explained she kept having dreams about two teen-agers who had been missing for almost two years. She wanted to see if I picked up on anything from the place.

I felt nothing as I walked around the property. I talked with her for a while and told her I had to leave. Before I could leave, Jean insisted that I hear her out concerning these kids. She handed me an article that appeared in her local paper about Rachel and Franklin Hartman.

According to the newspaper article, Rachel and Franklin Hartman were last seen with their father, Gordon, as they were leaving the fireworks display on July 4th, 2003, in Concord, New Hampshire. Witnesses recalled seeing the three walking toward their minivan at approximately 10:00 p.m., and their recollections were unquestionably vivid since all three Hartmans were in the midst of a very heated public argument. Gordon was upset with Rachel for not meeting him at the predetermined location following the event, and Franklin took the somewhat rare position of defending his older sister. By all accounts, the boy usually sided with his father. The debate was intensified by Gordon's apparent disgust that Rachel had not properly charged her cell phone, thereby inhibiting his ability to reach her some fifty yards away.

The newspaper article stated that Rachel's boyfriend, as well as other friends, made repeated calls to Rachel's cell phone and home number on Saturday, July 5, but no one was able to reach her. She had plans for a sleepover on that Saturday, and most certainly never went a day without talking to her boyfriend. While it was certainly unusual, there wasn't necessarily a need for panic until the next day. The Hartman children were parceled out between their parents for a time after their divorce. Melinda, the children's mother, was due to pick up Franklin on Sunday afternoon, July 6, for two weeks of summer camp. There was no great need to worry when they were not there, as the normal exchange took place on Sunday evenings. Perhaps Gordon forgot about being there for Franklin's camp.

On Monday, July 7, after no word from her ex-husband or children, Melinda placed a call to Gordon's employer and found out that Gordon had been terminated from his job three weeks earlier. Employment was a necessary condition of their custody arrangement and he had not shared this development with anyone, let alone Melinda.

Still unable to reach either Gordon or Rachel on their cell phones and fearing the worst, Melinda sought and obtained a court order on Monday, July 7, revoking Gordon's custody rights and compelling him to return the children. This formality enabled the police to treat the incident as a crime and a missing persons case.

Authorities tracked down Gordon by following the activity on his credit card. He was found at a hotel in California on July 10, six days after he was last seen with the children and three days after the formal complaint had been filed. He was arrested without incident and placed in custody by California and Federal authorities. Of great concern was the fact that Gordon had stopped at a Pennsylvania Wal-Mart on the morning of July 5 and purchased a shovel, a pickaxe, black garbage bags, duct tape, a knife, and other items. Of greater concern was that Gordon was apprehended alone and in possession of two handguns. What was most disturbing was that Gordon's minivan contained a great deal of blood, human tissue, and bullet holes covered with duct tape.

I continued reading the article and promptly realized this wasn't a "who done it" type of case but a "where done it." Once he was under police custody, Gordon confessed to the murder of his two children. He shot Rachel in the head once and Franklin several times in the chest shortly after they left the fireworks in New Hampshire. Hartman buried his children in shallow graves with duct-tape crosses upon their chests sometime on July 5, 6, or 7. Federal authorities gathered very detailed information from Gordon about a burial site that he said was within two to ten miles of an unidentified exit from Interstate 80 somewhere in the Midwest. The remainder of his trip became an effort to clean the van, dispose of all the evidence, and apparently restart his life all while continuing to use his credit cards, ATM card, and even wire transferring thousands of dollars from a home equity line of credit back in New Hampshire.

Over the course of the next several days, law enforcement officials drove Gordon through Pennsylvania, Ohio, and Iowa, making several stops along the way whenever Gordon seemed to remember where he had potentially dug the two shallow makeshift graves for his children. I was feeling horrified and disgusted by the callousness of this man but I wanted to help. I wanted to help Jean, the kind woman who first contacted me; I wanted to help the children's mother, Melinda, even though I didn't know her yet; and most of all, I wanted to help those children by bringing them back home.

When investigators failed to find the precise location or the bodies, Gordon was formally extradited to New Hampshire three days later and charged with the murder of his children.

Thus far, and despite countless hours of searching for their remains, neither Rachel's nor Franklin's bodies were found. In an ironic turn of events that voided prosecutorial value in finding the children, Gordon, the only individual presumed to know the exact location of the graves, committed suicide in jail while awaiting his trial. The children's mother, her family, friends, and their small New England community were devastated by the tragedy.

A website was created in the hope that someone would recollect an important detail either about that fateful night in Concord, or more importantly, a familiarity with the burial site located somewhere between Pennsylvania and Iowa that holds the bodies of young Rachel and Franklin.

I decided to take on the case and started by asking Jean for the mother's phone number so I could call her and ask if my delving into the disappearance of her missing children for the purpose of finding their whereabouts would be okay with her.

I called Mel, as friends and family call her, and she gave me the green light. She asked if there was a way I might be able to really find her kids. She added that at this point she knew they were already dead.

Over the next few months I spoke with Mel several times, and she asked me to check out several areas because she had received some tips about them. I did check the areas but felt no connection there and reported this back to her. This case was now haunting me day and night; I just couldn't let it go. I thought about it constantly and drove over the turnpike to get a feel for the father's vibration that he left when he was at the site to see if I could locate the exact spot.

As I drove along the highway, I picked up his vibration. I had realized that after talking to Mel, I was able to hone in on Gordon's vibration. I grabbed my cell phone to call Jean. I asked her if she ever heard of Ohio State Route 8 and she replied, "Why yes! It's near Hudson, Ohio. I have family near there." I said, "Jean, I think I located the city [where the children are buried]." Jean was overjoyed, and then I told her that I would need to plan a trip to the area. Jean said, "I will help you map out your trip if you want me to," and I told her that since she was so familiar with the area, this would be a great help to me. Several days later I picked up the maps from her.

In August 2005, I called Mel and told her I was sure that the kids were in the state of Ohio and near a city called Hudson, which is on State Route 8 and not too far from Route 303, where I had seen a vision of Gordon lost on that route. I told her that I was planning a trip to the area to investigate and see if I could feel a connection to the children.

In October, 2005, I drove the four hours to Hudson, where I met a friend of Mel's named Ed. His kids and Mel's kids went to school together and he wanted to help. We drove around and through several cities near Hudson so I could pick up Gordon's vibrations and get a feel for where he had driven. Like profilers refer to the MO of a perpetrator, I refer to these vibrations as a person's signature. They are like fingerprints, and no two are alike. The electrical vibrations can linger for up to five years or so after the person has been in a location or an area. I traced Gordon to several areas but couldn't pinpoint where the children might be located. I drove home for more meditation on the exact location. One week later I sent an email to Ed and Mel to tell them that I felt the kids' exact location was on a road near Hudson. I could not go there right then due to ice storms in our area, but I told her to send this out to the media in Hudson to get help from the local people. On December 1, 2005, Franklin and Rachel Hartman's bodies were found on the exact road I had mentioned, off Route 8 in Hudson, Ohio, just as I had told them they would be. A woman who had obtained the information from my website and from all the local media went to the area and found them. They were buried in very shallow graves, and the plastic and duct tape were visible and had caught her attention. She called the police and they recovered the bodies, which were later positively identified as Rachel and Franklin.

I only spoke to Mel on the phone once after her children were found. She told me she could not tell anyone that she had used the services of a psychic because her church would frown upon it. Jean called me to tell me she was glad I found the kids and that she can rest easy now that they are finally at peace.

Chapter 9

THE PLATEAU

In mid-December, 2005, a television station staff from Japan who had heard about me from my appearance on *Larry King Live* contacted me via email. They wanted to know if I would be willing to try to find a missing local woman whose name was Yumiko. The case was very well-known all over Japan so the pressure was on. The television station would pay for my trip overseas, and I said yes.

The initial email the television station sent included a photo attachment of the missing woman. She was beautiful and had the sweetest face. I could see the love she had in her eyes, but they also conveyed a deep sorrow. As soon as I saw the photograph, I began to hear the word "plateau." I had no idea what that meant or how it would fit in.

When I talked to the interpreter for the television station on the telephone, I told her I kept hearing the word "plateau." She said she didn't know what it meant and had to look it up.

The interpreter called me back the next day and said the area where the family lived was called the Inashiki Plateau, which was located in a small village outside of Tokyo.

The television station also faxed me the following information in order for me to gain a background on the case:

Around 10:30 p.m. on December 13, 2005, Yumiko changed into her pajamas. She went to her room and went to bed, as usual. The next morning, around 7:30 a.m. on December 14, Sakura, her mother, went to Yumiko's room to wake her up. But all she found was an open window and no sign of her daughter.

When her mother went to search for her outside in the field connected to their backyard, she saw footprints that appeared to belong to Yumiko. The footprints led up to a nearby bamboo grove. Since the soil in the field was very soft, it outlined an imprint of a foot, including the big toe, suggesting that Yumiko was not wearing shoes or socks at the time of her disappearance. But that morning it had been brutally cold, the temperatures dropping to -6°C (-25°F). In fact, it was so cold that the footprints had frosted over.

Yumiko's family was very surprised at her disappearance and requested that the local fire company search for her. That day, around ten people initially went on the search. Her family also requested police help. The next day, December 15, around seventy people, including neighbors and firefighters in a nearby town, also joined the search, fanning out approximately a mile from the house. However, they did not find any leads that pointed to the disappearance of the young woman.

I went overseas to Japan in January 2006. Right before I boarded the plane, I pulled out Yumiko's photo. The words, "Look up, look down!" kept coming to me. I thought to myself, "Are you losing it?" I was doubting what I was hearing and was not understanding the information I was receiving in regard to Yumiko's disappearance.

As soon as I arrived in Tokyo, the authorities provided me with more information about the missing girl. We then drove to the village and to the Yumiko's house.

When I entered Yumiko's room, I felt I needed to go outside her window; a force was pulling me there. I began to walk outside and continued on my journey through a bamboo grove and across the street to another small road. I felt her vibration very strongly at this time.

I began to sense that something was very wrong and stopped in my tracks. I had a vision of a tree, and when I looked closely at the tree, I saw a man hanging from the tree. This overwhelmed me at first and I took my time before saying this to the television station director and the crew. The family of the missing girl was in the house, but not outside in the road with us at that particular time. When we went back to the house and I told the family what I saw, they confirmed what I was seeing. There was a tree at that location but it was cut down two years ago because Yumiko's brother hung himself from that tree.

I continued to stroll through the bamboo grove and walked across the street to another small road. I felt Yumiko even more strongly at this time. I accelerated my pace to an almost running speed, and the camera crew was running after me, trying to keep up. About half a mile down the road, I came to a small cemetery, although I did not know at the time what the place was since their burial places are very different from ours. We have headstones but they have shrines, and some of them are huge. This particular cemetery was a private plot for just their family.

As I stood there, I could feel Yumiko's presence. I asked the producers about their prior searches with police. They said they had searched several areas. "They missed her," one of them said. Another replied, "No, because they had dogs." I said to the director, "She was missed, but she was there."

This area was filled with slopes. I began to get the sense that Yumiko was laying on one of them. I walked up a hill and felt tears running down my face and a sense of deep loss. I touched one of the shrines and said, "This is the father's grave," and then pointed to the one next to it. "And that one belongs to the brother."

When the interpreter told the crew what I said, they truly looked as though they had seen a ghost. Then they confirmed what I had said, that those were indeed the father's and the brother's final resting places. I then told them Yumiko had been to this place several times on the day she disappeared.

Meanwhile, the film aspect of this investigation was crazy. We had to do many different takes, and I was afraid we were losing valuable daylight with all the time being wasted with retakes. I started to walk into a grove of various trees, including bamboo. I walked another half-mile up a hill and I came across an abandoned car in the woods. I touched the car for several minutes while the filming crew looked baffled. I turned to them and said, "This is a friend of the brother. He is dead also. He killed himself too."

It was getting dark, and it was time to drive back to Tokyo. We went back the next morning to see the girl's mother. The mother and I greeted each other and spoke through an interpreter. She cried and hugged me and begged me to help her find her daughter. She thanked me profusely for coming to Japan to try and find her daughter. This was a very emotional meeting for both the mother and me.

We did some more filming at the news studio on the following day and I described the area where Yumiko's body could be found. I was seeing a vision of the location and described what it looked like to the television crew. "It is a tall, grassy area with spring flowers. There are one or two cherry trees nearby. I can see and smell water. The water seems to come from some sort of irrigation. It is on a slope!" I realized at that very moment why I kept hearing "Look up, look down!" before I boarded the plane. I was supposed to look for a slope. I told the television crew that Yumiko would be found in an area one-half mile east from her home in an area that had already been searched. I also said her body would be difficult to find, and she would be found the first week of April. My visit took place in January.

Two months went by after I had returned home and I hadn't heard any news in regard to Yumiko's recovery. I received a call from Japan during the first week of April informing me Yumiko had been found in the area I described, with an irrigation system and all. Her mother was on the phone and she wanted to thank me.

The minute I heard the mother's voice, I saw visions of rabbits and flowers. I heard the voice of Yumiko. She was saying, "Thank you. Thank you for the pink." I did not understand this, but I relayed it to the interpreter who in turn informed the mother of what I said. The mother let out a wail that made me feel as though I should have kept my mouth shut. The mother told the translator that she had placed two pink stuffed bunnies and pink flowers in front of her daughter's picture the day before.

"The World's Most Astonishing News" devoted a segment to this story and my uncovering of evidence, and it was aired in all news channels in Japan on Asahi TV and Nippon TV.

I felt saddened by the outcome of Yumiko's disappearance, as I often do, but relieved that her mother finally knew where her daughter was and could be at peace.

--- Chapter 10 ---

WHERE IS THE GOOD DOCTOR?

When a person goes missing, the local media goes into overdrive and saturates the residents with information. When a very attractive young man went missing in Columbus, Ohio, I saw his photo every day on television or in the newspaper. Ben was a twenty-seven-year-old, second-year medical student at Ohio State University who went missing in April 2006. He was last seen on April 1 with some friends at a local sports bar popular with young people. It is a clean-cut place that caters to the local college students.

I couldn't avoid all the information about Ben that was coming at me through the media. I prefer not to know anything about a case beforehand, but it was next to impossible to not hear about this case. From various accounts and tips flooding the police hotline, Ben was last seen going up an escalator to the sports bar near the university. The security camera verified that Ben went into the bar but that was the last time anybody saw him. Ben had vanished, as they say, without a trace.

It was close to spring break, which is the time when college students go wild. For medical students like Ben, spring break is a welcome respite from the rigorous studies their careers demanded. Apparently Ben went to the saloon to celebrate and relax with friends, but how could he possibly have disappeared?

Detectives from Columbus traveled to six states and to the U.S. Virgin Islands to follow up on leads, but failed to turn up any evidence or information in regard to Ben's disappearance.

There were no leads and no suspects. Central Ohio Crime Stoppers was offering a $25,000 reward for any information that could lead to Ben's whereabouts. A television reporter stated that, according to police, a homeless man said he had recently seen Ben behind a United Dairy Farmers store, located at High Street and 12th Avenue.

"The individual indicated that the man he had seen was eating a sandwich," said the Columbus police detective. "He believes it was bought from one of the local restaurants."

Detectives said the homeless man attempted to talk with the man he believed was Ben, but the person walked off into the alley.

"(The homeless man) said that he said, 'Hey, people are looking for you,' and the individual really didn't have much of a reaction," the detective said.

Ben's mother died shortly before he disappeared. His father, Barry, believes the loss of his mother, with whom Ben was very close, added to the pressure of his studies, might have been a catalyst for his conscientious son to make the decision to simply disappear. Apparently the father was mostly seeking solace in the possibility that Ben was still alive and gone of his own free will.

"It hasn't been totally checked out yet, but I am going with that positive thought," Barry said. "It lifts me up a little bit."

Clyde Ferris, Ben's roommate, was the last person to have seen him alive. He stated that Ben is someone who is known to go and do his own thing. Clyde provided the following timeline in a blog forum dedicated to finding Ben.

The men headed to the sports bar at about 9:15 p.m. At about 10:30 p.m., Ben spoke to his girlfriend over the phone. About thirty minutes later, the men walked to a nearby tavern, where they had a few drinks. At 11:40 p.m., they walked to another bar. At about 1:15 a.m., they returned to the sports bar. Clyde said while he was drinking, Ben periodically walked away to talk with some people he knew.

"Ben got up with them. I am assuming he got up with them and walked out with them to talk with them on the foyer before going on the escalator," Clyde said.

Ben was last seen on surveillance cameras at about 2:00 a.m.

"I called him that night and it went straight to voicemail. It was about 2:00 a.m. and [there was] no answer," Clyde said.

He stated he did not think Ben had a nervous breakdown. "I am afraid that Ben might have left the bar and ran his mouth a little bit. He has been known to do that," Clyde said.

At closing time, after looking for Ben, Clyde said he went home with another friend. "Of course, now I regret leaving, but I didn't think anything of it then. I didn't think Ben—that anything happened to him because he is known to walk away." Ben had made definite plans for his overdue vacation from med school. He and his girlfriend were scheduled to take a spring break trip to Florida, NBC 4 reported. Police said that none of his bank or credit cards had been used since he disappeared.

After a year of being barraged with all the information of Ben's case, I thought maybe I should check it out and see if I could find Ben. I quietly and discreetly began to check out different areas. I started with a blind drive around the sports bar when Ben was last seen. I was able to pick up his vibration. I was able to follow it and found where he was living. I picked up a lot of information and then I lost him. I told my daughter Tamra, "Maybe we should just drive around and see what we can pick up."

I started driving all around the city and downtown area until I came across a road called Mound Street. I knew this street had some significance to Ben. My friend Brian has prophetic dreams and draws what is shown to him in the dreams. I sent some maps to him to see if he could pick up on anything in regard to Ben's disappearance. He had drawn a map in his dream drawing that pointed to the same area.

I felt like I was driving in circles in Columbus because I just wanted to feel something. I began to pick up some things surrounding Ben near the Siota River. There were a lot of homeless people who stay in the park near the river where I was picking up on Ben's vibration. I felt it was dangerous for Tamra and me to be there by ourselves. We decided we needed to back off and come back later when we had more people and time, being that it was starting to get dark.

The following week I went back to the same area with a couple of people from the Columbus area who knew the area and Ben's story. We walked along the embankment near the river. It was so steep along the entire river that it was going to be quite a task to look for bones. The river is so fast with such a terrible undertow that I don't know that a body would surface. I do know that if he fell in, there is no swimming out of there. Whoever falls in the river is a goner. The movement of the river was so fast that I could hardly hear myself.

We met a homeless man and talked to him. We showed him a picture of Ben and asked if he had seen the young man and if there had been any strange activity in the area. He laughed and said that there was strange activity back there all the time. However, the homeless man said he had not seen Ben. He gave us a warning and said, "If you come back here, come and get me because it's not safe."

When I first started investigating Ben's case, his dad, Barry, did not know I was doing this. A producer who was working on the show *Psychic Kids* called me, and said, "You're one of the most well-known psychic detectives and we know you've done shows on A&E and Court TV. We wondered if you'd do a show with *Psychic Kids* and introduce the kids to a missing persons case because they usually deal with the paranormal."

I agreed and told them that I would like to focus on Ben's case. If the families don't come to me, I work alone without contacting anybody. I feel we are not credible if we are out there preying upon the families. The producer contacted Barry and asked if he would be willing to participate along with the psychics in a show that focused on his son's case, and he said of course he would.

I was at the sports bar where Ben was last seen during the filming of another psychic television show. I picked up on Ben's vibration and went out the emergency exit door. I expected the alarm to sound, but it didn't go off. I couldn't figure out how he got out of there, but maybe it was through this door. I had a feeling he left with someone who had business there. I felt he left willingly, but had no idea what happened to him. Sometimes the timing is not right to find the missing person. People think if one is a psychic, one can always bring them home, but I'm not divine providence.

Barry was hurting deeply when I first met him during the filming of the television show. He had lost his wife, he had lost his son, and his father died after Ben disappeared. It was a constant pain for him, but he was a very genuine, very caring person. In all the years I've been working on missing cases, I don't think I have met a kinder person than Barry. I cried with him. We talked on the phone because he knew I understood what he was going through. Sometimes he'd call me out of the blue and say, "I'm feeling down today, Gale. I don't think we're ever going to find Ben." I said to him, "I promise you, Barry, if it's the last thing I ever do, I'm going to try to bring Ben home. I will never stop searching for him."

There was a windstorm on September 14, 2008. It killed two men, including Barry. He was only fifty-five. It seems that Barry was walking to a shed in his backyard when he was struck by a large limb of a tree. I don't know how many times

I cried over Barry's death. This is one of the few times I found myself saying, "Why, God? Why?"

I have not been back to the area since Barry passed away, although I do want to go back to look for Ben. The main reasons I haven't been able to go back and continue searching are finances and personal things in my life that seemed to get in the way, but recently Barry has been on my mind. The only way I can explain it is that some things are shifting. I feel something is going to happen and that maybe Ben is ready to come home. I can't say how soon because I don't know. I just feel that shift coming.

I remain extremely frustrated with the case of Ben and have shed many tears over it. That case became very personal to me. It became personal the first time I was there. I didn't know why, but it made sense when I met Barry. I feel very driven to find Ben, and I know that one day he will be found.

Chapter 11

LOST LITTLE BOY

I had made many kindhearted and well-meaning friends in Florida while I was there searching for a missing girl, and they enlisted my help in the disappearance of a young, mentally handicapped boy and provided me with a place to stay. Cases that involve children affect me more than adults, and when I learned more about the case and saw a photo of the missing boy, I knew I had to head to Florida and pursue the case.

My friends sent me a poster that had been distributed in the area that listed the following details.

January 10, 2009
Immokalee, Florida

Adbul has been missing from his grandmother's residence in Immokalee, Florida, since Saturday, January 10, 2009, at approximately 5:30 p.m. Abdul reportedly went outside to play with neighborhood kids after dinner. He was reported missing a little while later and his whereabouts remain unknown.

Abdul was last seen wearing a blue and yellow t-shirt, blue and yellow shorts, and black and gray sneakers. He is mentally handicapped and functions at a two-year-old level. He is nonverbal, has a very limited vocabulary, and only understands Creole.

When I first looked at the photograph of Abdul, I got the impression that there was a lack of understanding in the smiling little boy's face. I didn't know if it was due to his language barrier or a mental challenge.

I felt I had a really good idea of what had happened to Abdul, and I felt very strongly that I needed to go to Florida and see what I could discover in regard to this case.

There was already a buzz about the case in the area before we even arrived. The *Naples News* reported our arrival in the area:

A nationally-known psychic is heading to Southwest Florida to do her part in the search for Abdul. Psychic Gale St. John was slated to arrive in Immokalee Wednesday night and will start searching today for 6-year-old Abdul, who has been missing from Farm Workers Village since Jan 10. In an interview, St. John said she would be arriving at Orlando International Airport Wednesday afternoon and then she'd drive to Immokalee. 'Everything is taken care of,' said St. John before catching her flight to Florida. 'We have a place to stay.'

However St. John, who is traveling with her daughter Tamra, said she has not reached out to Abdul's family. 'We don't seek out the family to bother them,' she said, adding that she respects the family's privacy, but that they should feel free to contact her.

Also unaware of St. John's pending visit—the Collier County Sheriff's Office. 'We were unaware of her visit,' said the sheriff's office spokeswoman, adding the department has had no contact with St. John. 'But we will be trying to contact her.'

The sheriff's office spokeswoman added that law enforcement was open to any ideas that would assist them in locating the missing little boy.

Tamra and my friend Galena, whom I had met on my previous visit to Florida, accompanied me on this case. Galena lived in the area and graciously allowed me and Tamra to stay at her place.

When I started my first blind drive in the area, it was a combination of feeling and knowing that Abdul had crossed through an area that seemed like a gate to me. It felt like the land that time forgot. I had first picked up on this impression when I was back home and looking at Abdul's photo. When I went to Florida to investigate, I discovered that in a sense where he had gone missing was a place that time forgot.

One of the newsmen who had read about my arrival in the paper was accompanying Tamra, Galena, and me during the first blind drive so he could see what would happen. I told him, "First of all, I can't be responsible if I make a really sharp turn or come to a screeching halt. Secondly, please be quiet." He laughed and complied. He was a good sport and a good reporter.

We walked back into an area where we had to cross a drainage ditch. There were alligators in the water; I could see their tails poking up through the water's surface. Alligators can hide in just one foot of water, and although attacks on people are rare, they have occurred. I personally don't think it's a good idea to incur their wrath by stepping on the head of one of the beasts. We put a board across the ditch to keep us from sinking into the muddy sand, but we were still ankle-deep in the water. I thought, "What the hell am I doing?" The gators were laying there as if it were siesta time.

The path went through an orange grove and led to a vast area that was a cross between an orange grove and garbage dump, and that included a few trailer houses. It was a sad, desolate area, not to mention the fact we were all very nervous. We spotted a wild boar, and the gators in the drainage ditch had unnerved us. We walked through a grassy area, and Galena said, "Oh my God! It's a gator!" The gator was about fifteen feet long. I took a deep breath and swallowed my heart back down because it was up in my throat. I said to Galena, "And we both thought it was a grassy path. Uh oh." Immokalee is like the Everglades. It is not land covered with grass; it's all swamp with deep water below it. On top of it all, it was gator mating season! Galena said, "So what the hell do we do?" I told her, "We can try to spook the gators." We did spook them by making loud noises and they thankfully went away.

We walked through the orange grove/garbage dump and found a grove of banana trees. As we got close to them, Galena collapsed into a hole. Holes are where alligators stash their kill. I jokingly said, "Leave her there! Hey guys, have lunch for a while!" Thankfully Galena has a wonderful sense of humor, but when she climbed out of the hole, I noticed Tamra was in tears. She was very upset by the gators and wildlife we had experienced so we called it a day and headed back to Galena's house.

Before we started the third blind drive through the area, Galena said, "Let's make this real and blindfold you." I had never done this before, so I agreed, "Okay I'm all for it." Galena drove around the area to make sure I didn't know where we were starting. We did the blind drive twice with the blindfold and Galena made sure we started from a different place on the new drive so that I didn't know from where we were starting.

We found the house where Abdul's grandmother lived during one of the drives. I knew it was not where he was, but it was an important location. Galena said, "This is where he stayed with his grandmother when she babysat him."

I said, "Okay, let's move on." I kept saying, turn, take this street, or stop. I would explain what I was feeling in different areas. Tamra said, "Galena, I hope you know where you're going because I have no clue." It didn't matter where we began, but every time I ended up directing us to an abandoned blue house.

We got out of the car and walked around to see if I could pick up on anything. We saw a little girl playing outside and I thought we should go talk to her to see if she knew anything about Abdul's disappearance. We walked over and I asked her, "Hey, you know about the little boy who went missing?"

She said, "Oh yeah, we were playing and I got called in to dinner and the two other little boys were called in as well, so Abdul was here all by himself."

I asked, "How did the other kids take to Abdul playing with them?"

She said, "They didn't like him and they were mean to him. They would hit him and knock him down. He didn't have any friends."

I asked her how the adults reacted to this behavior.

"Well, if my Grandma had found out I was talking to you she would have had a fit because we speak Creole." She said the adults didn't pay attention to what was going on because they were working. There wasn't a whole lot of supervision.

We could see a metal gate that led into the orange grove area in the distance. I said, "Instead of trying to get killed by a gator, let's get in the car and go over there." We found a little road that led to the metal gate, which was open, so we drove the truck right on through and checked out a trailer and shed. I wasn't getting any feelings at all.

Galena said, "Let's go farther down this road."

The feelings got stronger as I got closer to the house.

Galena suggested that I go into a trance.

We drove back through the gate and found a shady spot with a big tree near a church. I had never gone into a trance meditation in a vehicle, especially in this heat, but after a few tries I was able to go into a trance. The information I received was about the distance we had to go, some distance to a hill, in an area that was ranch-like. I got information about a pipe, which I didn't understand. We thought we should go back to the area through the gate where we had just been.

One of my guides said, "You can't," and I relayed the info to the others.

Galena asked, "Why can't we?"

The guide said, "It's locked."

I came out of the trance and we decided to go back there, and of course the gate was closed and locked, just as the guide had told me.

Galena said, "You know what? That will teach me not to argue with spirits. We could have gotten locked in there in the truck."

I did several blind drives on this case and ended up in the same place each time: the abandoned blue house. The drainage ditch and orange grove we'd gone through on the first blind drive is directly in back of this house. I also received information from my friend Brian. The area described to me was nearly the same as the one I explored. He told me what he saw in his dream: "I saw water and orange groves, gators, and a blue house. You need to go behind that house to get to this area. I saw a dog, and followed it. This area was known to the boy, as many kids went back there from time to time."

I couldn't guarantee this is where the boy disappeared, but I was more than willing to search the area. The Florida law enforcement officers told me it had already been searched. I spoke to the detective in charge of the case and gave him the information I had but he did not seem to take it seriously. He assured me they would get dogs out there. About a month after Tamra and I returned, Galena went back to the area where we had directed the officers to search. She talked to the neighbors and the local papers. Nobody had been out there. As of today, Abdul is still missing. Cases like this are frustrating, but I hope one day this little boy will finally be found.

--- Chapter 12 ---

WHAT REALLY HAPPENED TO LOUIE?

There are plenty of cases I have not been able to follow to their respective destinations because of time, distance, and money constraints. My friend Marta Sosa has an Internet radio show called *Cubanarama Missing N America*. She is a Cuban-American woman who lives in Minnesota and has made an avocation into a vocation to find the missing. I am her psychic consultant and we work well together, as she has a soft, sensitive touch with the families of the missing and departed. One case we tried to at least respond to together was brought to us by a former mafia wife.

Marta had been talking to Lynda Milito, the ex-wife of Louie Milito, a member of a powerful and long-standing mafia family in New York City. Louie had grown up in the city and was childhood friends with the people who formed and became kingpins of the particular family, so it was natural that he was welcomed into the mob family fold. Louie disappeared in 1988, and Lynda has been haunted ever since with thoughts of what really happened to her former husband and father to her children. A torso was found in 1990, but it was in the days before DNA testing, so Lynda and her children never had any closure or proof that Louie was dead. Lynda had been told by the head of the mafia family that Louie's childhood friend, Artie, told him that Louie was badmouthing the head of the family, which led to Louie's murder. Artie has denied that he was involved in Louie's death, but Lynda isn't convinced.

Before the radio show, Lynda gave Marta a rundown of the last time Louie had been seen. When Lynda and Louie's son was seriously injured from a motorcycle accident, it took a toll on the marriage and they separated. Louie was staying at his friend Alberto's home, and on the last day he was seen, he was waiting for his daughter to meet him and go out for dinner. But before his daughter could get there, Louie received a phone call. When he got off the phone he told Alberto that he had to leave and to tell his daughter he could not wait for her. This was the last time Louie was seen. No one knows who that call was from and where Louie went or whom he went to meet that was more important that his dinner date with his daughter. When Lynda spoke to her daughter, the daughter said Louie never met her at the restaurant for dinner. Lynda then asked their son, who was in a body cast from his accident, if he had heard from his father. No one had heard from him, and all of Louie's friends gave his former wife and family the runaround.

Marta invited Lynda and me to be on her radio show, and shortly before the program started a whole bunch of information suddenly came rolling into my head. It comes in very fast so I was trying to convey what I was seeing and try to make sense to Lynda as I was rattling off what I was seeing. I saw two brothers in a restaurant. I asked Lynda who owns the restaurant, who are the two brothers, and who are Giovanna and Joe. "There are a lot of characters involved, but I'm going to tell you something," I told Lynda. "There are two families involved. This is all like *West Side Story*. They are only related through marriage, not blood." The impression I got was that Louie got too big for his breeches and the other side of the family took him out.

When the radio show with Marta and Lynda began, I repeated what I heard and saw. Lynda confirmed the restaurant, which was an Italian place where Louie and his cronies would meet in the back of the restaurant. I also heard the name Al. Lynda said it was someone nicknamed "Ally Boy." I saw two brothers who were both in the Mafia and involved in Louie's disappearance. I saw that "Ally Boy" also had something to do with this. I also felt that Artie did not do the dirty work on this, but he did call the meeting and set this up. The trigger man was a man trying to make his place in the Mafia. Louie's death was a slap in his face during his final hour, because I feel while Artie might not have been the trigger man, he was there to look Louie in the face before he died. Artie needed to climb this ladder by himself and Louie was in his way. Artie wanted it all. It turned out Artie never climbed that ladder because he was caught for other crimes and ended up in jail, so nothing went according to plan for Artie.

I do believe the torso that was discovered is Louie's. No one seems to know where this torso is at the moment, and everything that could have been used to identify the torso at the time was not used. This seems very suspicious and smells of a cover up.

Chapter 13

WHEN A CHILD SUFFERS

These are probably the cases that affect me the most, and when I feel the greatest drive to solve them. A four-year-old boy went missing when he was walking to his aunt's house next door. This case was brought to my attention via Brian. All he gave me was the child's name and age. I saw a man who was involved with this child and told Brian I thought the man was lying concerning the whereabouts of this little boy. Then I was shown the death symbol. In some cases I am not always shown this symbol, but in this case it was shown to me in two different ways.

There are two ways in which I see death: if I look at a photo of the missing person, I see death when there's a dark circle around them. Since I did not see a photo of this little boy, I was shown a black rose. Other people who have the ability might be shown a different symbol, but this is what was shown to me. I then saw an area of woods not far from the area where the boy lived. I also heard the last part of a word and was not sure of the first part. The last sound in the word was *wick*. It was whispered to me, "wick, wick," and I couldn't make it out, but I could feel the closeness. Brian later told me that the boy's body was found in Renwick. I also felt there was some kind of evidence that a man disposed of evidence at his workplace, but this was never verified that I know of. Brian did some dream work on this and came up with similar things. As we followed this case we soon found out we were correct.

The details of the case were that the mother of the little boy had left her son in the care of her boyfriend, who had a long rap sheet of child abuse and had served time for abusing her older child. The boyfriend said the four-year-old boy was going to walk next door to his aunt's, and that was the last time he was seen. The search for the missing boy began in mid-December, and his remains were found the following March.

I told Brian there were several things that went on: the child was choked and beaten, and I feel that he was shoved into a bag while he was unconscious at that point, but still alive. I felt the bag was shut in a way that it cut off the air supply and the child's ability to breathe. I knew there was a lot of internal damage done to this little boy. I felt just sick. I was also very angry at the mother for trusting someone who had already done serious damage to one of her children. It is bad enough to kill somebody, but to make someone suffer the way this child suffered is unimaginable. As soon as I began that case I felt like I was going to vomit—I knew it was going to be bad. When someone dies quickly, it is not the same as when somebody suffers. When people die quickly I don't feel the same type of emotion. But, have you ever had the flu and feel like you're going to vomit up your insides? That is how it feels. It's the worst case of nausea, so I dread it when that comes over me. It had happened to me with a previous case in Florida, although not as bad as this.

The boyfriend was arrested for the murder of the little boy, and the case was tense and drawn out. The boy's blood was found in the house, and being that he had been sick during the day, the prosecutors established the boyfriend lost his temper and killed the little boy, stuffed him in a plastic bag, and then in a backpack, in which he was found.

The medical examiner testified that the boy died from a brain hemorrhage and that he suffered profound bruising to his buttocks and ankles before his death. She argued the personal injuries were typical of an adult seeking to punish, humiliate, and force submission on a child.

The defense's story often changed, and there was no alibi for the time when the boy went missing. The jury convicted the boyfriend of murder, and he was sentenced to fifty years in prison. It was heartbreaking this little boy had to die in the horrible manner he did, but I'm glad that justice was served in this case.

Chapter 14

FROM GERMANY WITH ANGST

This case was particularly interesting because it came to us via psychic detectives from Katmandu by way of Germany. The sister of a missing woman reached out to us in hopes to find information about her sister's whereabouts. Although several people were involved in the case and answered emails, all the answers came from me. One of my apprentices did make contact with Martha, the missing woman's sister, but the rest of the communication in this case was via email. The first email I received from Martha arrived in late 2005, not long after her sister went missing. The details of the first email are as follows:

Martha's thirty-one-year-old sister, Inga, who also lived in Germany, had left for vacation in August. She was traveling by herself throughout India, Tibet, and Nepal, and had planned to meet a friend at an airport in Tibet on October 18. Inga didn't show up at the airport, which was very unlike her typical behavior. The friend went to the hotel where Inga was staying and found out that all of her luggage, except a backpack used for day trips, was still in her hotel room. Inga's friend contacted the Nepalese police and the German embassy. During a search in the surrounding area, the police found a bra, vest, and hairclip that belonged to Inga. There were a few drops of blood on the articles, but there was no sign of Inga or the rest of her belongings. Martha was very distraught and wanted to know if we could help her discover whether Inga was still alive and why she was kidnapped.

I wrote back to Martha and said I felt that Inga was deceased and would be found within a half mile from where she disappeared, which I know didn't help since we didn't know exactly where she was when she disappeared. I felt that Inga would be found near a tree on a hillside downhill from a trail, like she had been dropped over the side of a hill. I said that I felt that Inga had been sexually assaulted, stabbed, and strangled. I sensed bruises on her throat. I also knew that Inga was not the first victim, and that there would be at least one more victim who will suffer the same fate as Inga.

Something that was very odd was that I felt that Inga did not pass away immediately. I felt that the person, and I only sensed one person who was acting alone, had been interviewed about her disappearance. I got the sense he was a park employee or worked for the forest service. Being that her belongings, spotted with blood, were found in the forest, I felt he had made himself very conspicuous in her search. I told Martha I felt he needed to be questioned again, and the name

Steven, Sten, or Sven kept coming to me when I tried to find a name.

We did not hear from Martha after I had sent the initial response, so when I received impressions from my other psychic team members, I sent another email with additional information. I told her that we all believed Inga was deceased, and that I was very sorry to pass along that information. We also felt that the person who did this to her had done the same thing to another female, who was around twenty years old, about a month or two before Inga disappeared, and that her body would be discovered near Inga's.

I said that my other team members reiterated the fact that she'd be found a half mile from where she disappeared, which is where her items were discovered. We all saw a valley, and she would be found on a steep hillside in this valley. I also sensed a cave or cavern that had been created by an earthquake. I very much sensed the area where Inga would be found was in an area that has active earthquakes.

We felt that the person who did this had since left the area, and that disappearances seemed to follow him wherever he goes. I had a feeling that he could possibly be in France and was still following the case and had possibly been in contact with law enforcement in regard to the case or had volunteered to lead a search. I knew he wasn't in the area anymore, but I felt he'd return in May and September. I sensed that he spoke at least three languages and was educated. Dhaulagiri was mentioned, like a name. I am not familiar with this word so we hoped that Martha would know what it meant.

One thing that I did pick up on that might help narrow down a location is that I saw an old building, like a shack or utility shed, or possibly an old bridge. This small building was in the same area where both women would be found. There might be brush on the hillside that is obstructing the view of the womens' bodies. I told Martha I hoped that helped in her search and asked for GPS coordinates so I could pull up a map and see if anything I saw on it triggered any more information as to Inga's whereabouts.

We were all in agreement that the man who committed these crimes had full and almost wavy dark-brown hair. He had a full beard and mustache that was full and fluffy, not wiry. His hair was short but not closely cropped to his head. It's fluffy around his face and down his neck a bit and covered his ears. He wore little rectangular sunglasses that are tinted orange. He was not fat, but his face was a little bloated and puffy, like he does not take care of his skin or his appearance. We felt he was a tourist or frequented the area, and that he was from Northern Europe. One of the team members felt that he had a fairly small build and Inga seen him before, and had possibly even spoken with him. But we felt that if there was some contact, it possibly was on a bus or some manner of public transportation. My initial impression was that it was one person, but some felt that possibly three could have been involved.

Martha wrote back and was very grateful for all of the information we had passed along to her and said she'd forward along the information to the authorities and ask around for a person like the one we described and with the name Steven, Sten, or Sven. They had not yet found the girls, even though there were cadaver dogs on the search. She wanted to know if the person responsible had ever lived in Thamel, which is the touristy place there.

Martha had forwarded along the GPS coordinates, and they did help us get a feel of the area, but we had a sense that they were searching south of the area where the bodies were located. I thought there was a possibility that Inga's things were planted there by whoever had killed her and the other woman.

Martha replied and said the German police couldn't find anything important near where Inga's items had been found, but that it was a difficult area to search, so if our team could be more specific as to where Inga would be found, Martha would pass the information to the Nepalese police and ask them to search the area.

I had to write back to Martha and tell her what she didn't want to hear, even though I had told her at the outset. It did not seem to have registered with her that her sister was dead. When I wrote to Martha, I told her that the man who killed Inga may be a climber from another country who travels to the area a lot. Dhaulagiri is a mountain that he has climbed before. He keeps coming back to that area because he knows the police won't be able to catch him there. I reiterated the information about the cave and that I felt he took her there after the first rape and struggle. He then took her to a jungle area and then to a steep valley where he dumped her body. He has killed before and there's a young girl with short hair who was killed a couple months before Inga and whose body will be found in the same area. The young girl is from a different country; I heard a different language from her. I also told her I sensed a watery area, not like a river, but something seasonal. Maybe a watering hole or an area that is prone to flooding. I urged Martha to have authorities look for a very deep cavern. I sensed there would be no more murders until May and/or September. I wasn't sure about that variance, but I believe he lived in France and that was when he planned to return to the area.

Angie is one of my psychic apprentices and directly wrote to Martha with what she was able to pick up on the case. After looking at some photos of Inga, Angie received a vision in her mind of Inga with a blue and white polka-dot bandanna around her head. Angie looked at the photos of Inga's belongings that were found in the forest, and she saw Inga in her bandanna. This was the validation that Angie's feelings and visions were correct and on the right track.

Angie saw a man with wavy brown hair who approached Inga in a very friendly manner. She may have missed a step and fallen and was crouching down as he came up. Inga was wary of him, and Angie felt he hurt her. Angie physically felt pain in the center of her chest and left kidney area, and she sensed that the man kneed Inga in those places. Angie also felt strain in her left shoulder and neck area, like someone grabbed her and pulled her up from the ground. Like the rest of us, Angie didn't feel that Inga was still alive, but that her body was still in the park, specifically in the northwest section of the park. Angie felt he dragged Inga behind some brush, and the soil was dry and very light in color, similar to sand. Inga's body was not buried, but would be found in an area full of brush.

Another team member passed along information to me that corroborated the details that Inga was in a steep ravine and there was an old building or bridge nearby, and that Inga was not the only woman who had gone missing from the area. Something different that came to that colleague was that possibly three men were involved, and that they do some kind of illegal business in the area.

I had passed along all the information we had gathered about the case, and I received a final email from Martha. She received word from the Katmandu police that a body was found and they believed it was Inga based on dental records and information as to what jewelry Inga wore. DNA tests would be conducted after the body was transported to Germany. Martha and her family were distraught, and even though I told her many times we felt that Inga was deceased, she still clung to the hope that her sister would be found. Now that Inga's remains had been found, Martha was faced with the harsh reality of her sister's death. We never learned if Inga's body was found in the cavern, nor do we know if anything was done to find the man who had murdered her. The body of the other young woman is also a mystery. It's very frustrating to not know all the details of the discovery of the body, as well as the thought that the person who murdered these young women is still out there, but at least Inga's body was found, and I feel that we were able to aid in its discovery. I hope that her family can move on from this tragedy.

Chapter 15

THE PARANORMAL

Marta Sosa, host of *Cubanarama Missing N America*, asked me to be on her show along with Celeste, the sister of slain Vegas dancer Debbie, who had mysteriously disappeared on December 12, 2010. Her dismembered body was later found in two plastic tubs, covered in cement, in an abandoned house. Debbie's boyfriend Mike and his roommate were arrested for her murder.

Celeste was a very soft-spoken young woman and sounded absolutely heartbroken over her sister's death. At first, Celeste seemed puzzled about the relationship between Debbie and Mike, who was also a dancer. At that point I felt things so strongly I had to jump in.

"I have to say this. Your sister knew very well this person would be the end for her," I said, and Celeste let out a sigh. I could have sworn she was silently crying. "But she couldn't stop her feelings," I continued. "It's like a drug addiction, she had to have it." Celeste was responding in agreement. I told her, "And she knew. She had visions of what was to happen. She had dreams and impressions but she put them off because her desire to have a relationship with this person was so much stronger than anything. It isn't necessarily that she felt she could change him as that she tried to accept him. The problem is he wasn't loyal to her."

Celeste said quietly, "No, he wasn't." I didn't know Mike nor anything about him, but I could see it all so clearly.

"And I don't mean four or five women, but many. There was no loyalty to her. She just wanted him to be kind and decent to her. And here is the sick thing: he didn't want anybody else to have her, even though he didn't want her, but he wanted her when he wanted her. She should just shut up and take it. She didn't have any problem saying when she was hurt, but he didn't care."

Celeste said, "I had that impression when I went out there." She immediately flew from Atlanta, where she lived, to Las Vegas when she first heard about her sister's disappearance.

Information was coming at me so fast, so I had to continue telling Celeste what I was picking up. "She had a good friend that he was with, and that really hurt Debbie. The affair with her friend caused a huge argument. Apparently he did drugs. The other girl liked to do drugs. Your sister didn't like drugs."

Celeste agreed, "No, she didn't. My sister didn't even drink."

I stated that Debbie's nature of not drinking or taking drugs caused a huge argument and Mike said a lot of unforgiving things. He pushed Debbie to the limit and she slapped him. Celeste was now sounding more energetic, more forthcoming.

At the beginning of the program, she sounded drained and depressed. Now she was articulate. "Everything you are saying makes perfect sense. I just wasn't a hundred percent sure."

"The whole situation was awful, but the day that it happened, that was the entire argument," I said, referring to the sinister final outcome.

Then Celeste volunteered, "According to the roommate, they were having an argument and Mike started to choke her. I know for a fact that she knew about another woman. Apparently the roommate tried to diffuse the situation, but then just left. When he came back, Mike had strangled my sister to death."

I clarified, "The thing is, she had the option to leave, but she was so angry she wanted him to give in and agree with her, but there was no reasoning with this guy."

Again, Celeste agreed, knowing her sister's temper. After a pause, Celeste did sound like she was crying when she asked, "Did she go peacefully?"

That is a very difficult question to answer, since I know exactly what the family member means by it. "You mean did she suffer? At the last minute she knew what was going to happen, but he held her against the wall. I would say yes, at the last minute she knew. He wasn't letting her have any air. She did suffer until the moment she passed out, but it was too late to think of why she stayed instead of leaving. Because when the roommate left, she thought of leaving." I felt awful. Celeste was sobbing quietly throughout all of this, but I had to tell her the truth of what I saw.

Marta wanted to know if Mike had planned Debbie's death. I replied that it was semi-premeditated in the sense he had feelings of wanting to hurt her before. He received a certain amount of pleasure from hurting Debbie, so he had thought about it. Mike had no remorse and was only sorry that he was caught.

Celeste relayed how Mike and his roommate placed her sister's body in a plastic tub and took it to a friend's house to see if she would store it.

"What happened was she was very small," Celeste prefaced, adding that Debbie was five f00t two. "What they did was put her into a plastic storage bin there and filled it with cement. They then took the bin to the home of a young woman who was friends with Mike. She asked what it was, and they didn't want to tell her, and Mike finally said, 'Debbie'. She didn't want to believe it. She told them to leave and take their gruesome cargo with them. As they were leaving the friend's house, apparently the tub cracked, so they took it to the abandoned house belonging to a friend. They came back with two new tubs and apparently that's when they decided to dismember her, put the tubs in a closet, and fill it with foam to hide the smell. The young woman in whose house they had tried to store the tubs had a friend who was in the police department and she led them to the body."

There were some questions back and forth as to whether the roommate would be charged as an accessory to the murder. What freaked me out was the control the ex-boyfriend could have had over his roommate. Mike was a very charismatic man and was able to project power and control over those around him. Marta had pointed out that Debbie was a very smart woman who had two degrees, including a doctorate, but she and Mike had such a powerful connection that was addictive. Debbie was becoming someone who wasn't anything like herself, and it's something that Celeste stated other boyfriends would not have been able to do or get away with.

I explained, "Sheer chemistry. It's something we barely understand. It's wow! You hope to someday have that relationship in your life, but when you have that much chemistry with a person, walk away! You want some chemistry, but not that addiction chemistry. It's like drugs; they're not good for you. She couldn't resist this drug."

We couldn't talk more about the case since it was an ongoing investigation and the trial had not taken place yet, so we moved onto the paranormal phenomena that Celeste had been experiencing since Debbie's death.

Celeste said she had heard sounds in her home and found objects out of place. Her dog barks at a chair when no one is sitting in it. Her baby babbles at the same empty chair. Celeste had brought her sister's belongings back to her home in Atlanta, and decided to put some of Debbie's items on the mantel.

"On this particular night my kids were not here. I was in my room and I heard something. I looked to see where the dog, a small Chihuahua, was. All her pictures on the mantel were knocked down. There wasn't an earthquake or a strong wind. They were laying toward the wall, so it was impossible for them to have fallen over."

I sensed a mischievous spirit and told her, "I know that when one says 'poltergeist' that's not nice, but it's her. It's very much your sister letting you know she's there. She's upset and angry, yet voicing her opinion as she did so well."

Celeste laughed, and was encouraged to go on, "On the morning of her memorial, I wrote some things down on a piece of paper and they just disappeared. Twice. The first time they disappeared I thought it was odd, but then the second time?"

Now it was I who laughed at this sibling relationship that was still going on.

"You should be able to wing it! Don't be so organized! She was organized, but she could give a speech in front of a hundred thousand people and wing it and give the best speech you ever heard."

Celeste laughed again and said, "Yes! Yes she could!"

I reassured her that there are so many things that come from the heart that cannot be written out beforehand, and that is what her sister wanted.

Celeste's voice broke a little bit as she asked, "Does she hear me sing to her?"

"Yes, yes she does."

Marta asked, "Does Debbie have a message for her sister and mom?"

I said, "This may sound like a cliché but she sends much love, but some things will come out. There was a book she was writing. You have to read between the lines."

Celeste replied, "I know she had several books, and I know she wrote a lot on her computer. She had several quote books that she highlighted."

I said, "There is a book she wrote very important things in. I feel she wrote about her own death."

Celeste asked about the lights in her home in Atlanta, which flickered on and off a great deal. "Is that her?" she asked.

I knew that, of course, it was. "She's been working on flickering the lights. There is a lot of fight in her. Give it to her, okay, because she's been working very hard on this. This is like learning to walk. So when those lights flicker, give it to her!"

That was one of the few moments Celeste laughed again.

Marta talked about a strange experience she had right before the time we were scheduled to do this show. She said she had heard very heavy rain outside her house. When she asked her daughter if it was raining, her daughter said no. Marta then felt heat come in the house from under the door. That is something that is not strange to me, and in fact is rather typical. I told Marta, "That is because they're letting you know they're there. They come to me before a show. When they talk to me at home at night, my boyfriend says, 'Are you talking to them again?' I tell him, 'If you don't see them, that's your problem!'"

We continued to talk and Celeste began to cry in earnest. It really broke my and Marta's hearts. "Does she know how much I love her and how much I pray?"

"Every day," I said, and I meant it. "She's here and she's saying it to me!"

I wanted to prove to Celeste that what I was saying was true, that her sister was right here with me, so I said, "I don't know what this means, but she really liked pink. She liked purple too, but the lavender purple not the gaudy purple."

Celeste was pleasantly surprised. "Yes, she loved pink and lavender! And I never liked them and I wear them now. All of a sudden I surround myself in purple and pink, and I never liked them before. Is there anything she wanted me to know in particular?" she asked me.

"This is going to sound strange, but a lot of people love roses. She hates them. She likes daisies."

Celeste came alive again. "Yes! She hated roses! She loved daisies!"

"And pearls, she is wearing pearls. She wants you to know that. Pink pearls!"

"Oh my God!" Celeste exclaimed. "Yes, she loved her pearls. She was never without her pink pearls!"

"These are things that are important to know so you know she's really here. The most important things are the things she impresses with you every day; the love and the comfort."

Marta wanted to talk about the upcoming trial, thinking perhaps Celeste ought to be able to draw some strength from this. I knew it wouldn't be easy for Celeste, but I got from Debbie that she didn't want what happened to her destroy what she was.

"What she's saying is it's not important what happens in the way of looking at her life. She's angry right now and she is saying, 'Everyone thinks I'm dead!' Her attitude is kind of dammit, don't let that destroy what I am. Take an item of hers with you, something pink or purple, and think of her today."

Celeste was crying again. "I talk to her every day like she's still here."

"That's what she wants. She doesn't want you to think about what happened. It's important to you and it's important to the court, but she's very headstrong."

Celeste, who would be at the trial of the murderer of her little sister every day, then asked, "Is there anything she wants me to say on her behalf?"

"It's very strange for me to say this, but she takes responsibility for her own actions that led to this. That is not to say that what happened is okay. She's very much saying I cannot give someone else a hundred percent of the blame. And I appreciate the fact she is like that. The most important thing she says is don't hold the grief and the anger because it will turn your life around. Turn it into a positive and not a negative. She keeps saying, 'own it.'"

Celeste said, "I have heard her say those words before."

"That means the grief and the anger, own it. That's how she describes the word. That way that person doesn't win. Are you the one that paints? Who paints?"

Celeste said, "I do."

"She'll come through you. Some artwork is coming from you because she is going to inspire you with beautiful things. And with work that will draw money and will help fund projects."

Celeste said, "Yes, I have been doing that, donating all the moneys to Shade Tree, a center for domestic violence. I also want her to know her friend Luke, who is a lawyer, is setting up a scholarship for arts and dance and music in her name."

I said, "Well, you and her friends are beginning to own it."

Mike is currently in jail in connection with Debbie's death. The roommate hasn't been implicated as of yet, but being that he provided testimony against Mike, he may have received a deal in regard to his punishment.

Chapter 16

CADAVER SCENTS AND DOG SENSE

I have always owned dogs or rather they have owned me. If you're a pet parent you know what I mean. I began working in earnest with rescue dogs in 2005 because I thought we would make a better team. I might be in the right area and be able to feel a presence, but the dog will be able to smell the scent of human remains.

Dogs have very acute senses, which is a proven fact, but I feel dogs can be just as psychic, if not more so, than humans. They are much closer to nature than us, and like wild animals, they sense storms and if they are becoming prey. We will never truly know how much ability they have.

Dogs have saved people in many circumstances. We have seen these amazing rescues in the news where the dogs have pointed to the culprits in not only murders, but also many arson investigations. There are many types of rescue dogs. Accelerant dogs are trained to pick up the scent of many types of accelerants and can detect the use of an accelerant after a fire. There are live find air scent dogs that specifically search for a live person's scent via air, and tracking and trailing dogs look for the trail that a specific person leaves behind using a scent article from the person they are looking for. Dogs that are often used in my line of work are specifically trained to pick up the scent of the decomposition of human remains.

When I decided to get my own search dogs, I wanted a breed that was good with people and had proven work ethics. After researching breeds, I settled on the Border Collie. I researched breeders that bred only working stock and no Border Collies for show dogs. I wanted the integrity of this breed kept intact. I would have preferred a shelter dog, and although there are many shelter dogs that have the drive to do this work, I would have to travel to a lot of shelters to find the right one. If I were testing a dog at a shelter I would have to throw a ball for the dog to retrieve many times and see if he gets distracted or if its only desire is to focus on the ball no matter what else is going on around it. I want a dog that wants that ball above all else, even if the world around him crashes. That's the kind of drive it takes to go on a search and reach an objective.

I found a woman who bred them in Brownstown, Illinois. When I called and told her what I wanted from the breed, she said my pup would be the half sister to a well-known avalanche rescue dog, so she felt there would be no issue training her for search and rescue (SAR). I got the pup when she was nine weeks old, and after watching her in action for a while, I named her Kimber after the gun brand. She would do her exercises as if shot from a gun; she was that quick and sharp.

Kimber. Courtesy of Gale St. John.

When Kimber was seven months old, I got a call from the breeder saying that her brother Simon had been returned due to his aggressive issues. He was a young dog so I found this hard to believe. The breeder said she thought he needed to be a working dog because of his drive. I paid the breeder $650, sight unseen. I had paid $750 for Kimber, which is cheap considering the cost of purebred Border Collies. Two weeks after I picked up Simon I took him to the trainer for the Indiana Search Team, of which I'm a member, and had him evaluated. He had scent training with me for two weeks and passed with flying colors. Kimber was evaluated after six months and passed as well.

Simon. Courtesy of Gale St. John.

Sooner than I expected, a new search pup came into my life and has been a wonderful addition to my hardworking dogs. Kindle is a Border Collie and shares the same hard work ethic as Kimber and Simon. She's a pup and I started her training right away, and after a short adjustment period she's taken to life as a search and rescue dog and part of our motley crew of dogs and cats.

Kimber and Simon came along with me when I went to pick up twelve-week-old Kindle from the breeder. Kimber was standoffish when Kindle first came into the room, and when Kindle put her feet on her, Kimber quickly let her know that that wasn't acceptable. Simon showed his teeth when Kindle approached him to show his displeasure with his new little sister. I immediately corrected them so Kimber and Simon knew that I meant business and that no matter how much they were annoyed by this new little pup, she was coming home with us. I then began some obedience work to calm the nerves of Kimber and Simon.

Kindle. Courtesy of Gale St. John.

The breeder raises her dogs around cats so the dogs are familiar with them in case they go to a home that has cats. I have two, Rebel and Chevy, so I was very glad that I didn't have to worry if Kindle knew how to act around cats. There are cats roaming all over the farm, and Kimber was in heaven when all the cats greeted her. It looked like she was grinning ear to ear, thinking "I am the Border Collie goddess!" When I opened up the door for Kimber to crawl in and head back home, about fifteen cats hopped in along with the dog. I expected her to say, "Can we keep them, Mom? Can we take them home with us?" No new cats came home with Kindle, but she has bonded so well with our cats, especially Chevy. They will curl up together and Kindle is so proud that she has her own cat.

Left to right: Kimber, Kindle, and Simon.
Courtesy of Gale St. John.

Simon had a hard time adjusting to our new life with Kindle. He was mean toward her and I could not leave the two of them alone. After four weeks of strife, Simon became more curious and kinder toward Kindle as she played with her toys. Simon loves playing with toys, so that was how he finally started to warm up to his new little sister. They are now wrestling buddies and get along just fine. She's a typical little sister, but our home is much more harmonious than those first few weeks.

You shouldn't be surprised to know that I'm going to get a fourth search and rescue dog from the same breeder. Being that I'm busier than ever with personal cases and helping with my search and rescue team, another dog will be a very welcome addition to my home.

Chapter 17

TRAINING

There's a big misconception about using search and rescue dogs. People think you just let the dog loose and it will go find the body. If only it was that easy! Training and working with search and rescue dogs, no matter if they are trained for live or human remains detection, is a huge commitment. It really is a fulltime job. I train with my team members two nights a week, and train the rest of the week at home or other locations. Simon is fully certified, but I still need to work with him every week to keep reinforcing his skills.

We must keep a written record of our training for legal and credential purposes for the state, and each dog must train at least four hours per week. I have three dogs, so I'm busy training them twelve-plus hours a week. All of my search and rescue work is volunteer. Many people give up because they don't realize the huge time commitment involved. I volunteer my time and my dogs to do whatever I can to help find missing persons. This is truly my calling, and I feel that I'm contributing to society by doing what I love. For me, it's all about right and wrong. I am as driven as my dogs to right the wrong that has been done and assist in finding victims and helping families find closure and peace. My hat is off to every handler and volunteer who works with search and rescue dogs. They are performing a great service along with their dogs. Training search and rescue dogs is no easy task, nor is it as black and white as you may think.

There are so many different variables that need to be considered. Scent is a very tricky thing, and here is where I will begin the explanation of scent and how it works.

First, let's talk about POD, meaning probability of detection. This is true of both live and human remains detection (HRD). While dogs can be used at any time of the day or night, they have a higher POD in the early morning and late afternoon to early evening. In the early morning, scent-generating particles that stopped decaying overnight will start emitting again when rehydrated by the dew and warmed by rising temperatures. Afternoon breezes will shear a vertically-rising scent plume and send the scent back along the ground. Scent emitting particles are most active in the late afternoon and early evening.

All humans, alive or dead, constantly emit microscopic particles bearing human scent. Millions of these are airborne and are carried by the wind for considerable distances. The air scenting SAR dog is trained to locate the scent of any human in a specific search area. The dog is not restricted to the missing person's track and can search long after the track is obliterated. Many air-scenting search dogs are also trained in trailing/scent discrimination.

Humidity and barometric pressure also have a large effect on how scent travels. I always check the levels before I start a search. One of the first things I do before embarking on a search is to take a bottle of baby powder and squeeze it. I watch the cloud of powder to see the direction of the wind in order to establish a plan of action.

As the handler I need to remind myself that the dog is only part of the team and that I need to be the brains of the operation and the dog is my nose.

When searching a small area I prefer to search into the wind, zigzagging back and forth into the wind. In larger areas we can search along parallel sweeps perpendicular to the wind. I must be thinking at all times and remember to search ridges when air is likely to be rising and down in drainages when air is likely to be falling.*

Training some of the other breeds may not be the same as training a Border Collie, for example. You can use most of the same methods, but you really need to keep in mind the characteristics of your breed of choice, mine being the quirky Border Collie. Being that my dogs are all Border Collies, I'll describe what I need to do in order to keep my dogs focused during training and during a search in the field. Simon and Kimber are trained strictly as human remains detection dogs. The HRD K9 is a dog that has been trained in the specialty of locating the scent of decomposing human tissue. The dog may be asked to locate a whole* corpse (as in a missing person

* Source: Jennifer Pennington, *Scent Theory* blog posting: *How Scent and Airflow Works, Hound and the Found.*

presumed dead), or only body parts from catastrophic trauma such as airplane crashes, or foul play with resultant body dismemberment.

This dog may also be taught to locate drowning or submerged subjects through either shoreline work and triangulation methods, or may work from a boat. When a person drowns, scent components (skin, particles, perspiration, skin oils, and other gaseous components) break down during decomposition and bacterial action and rise up through the water until they reach the surface. Once on the surface, the scent particles are dissipated by the breeze and current. A dog trained in water search can detect these scent particles and indicate to the handler the direction to the source in the same manner as an air scenting dog indicates scent during a wilderness search. This type of dog can be deployed on shore, but is better worked from a boat.

When I am in the woods searching for someone, the victim might have been there for ten or twenty years so the dogs needs to be specifically trained to find the remains. The first and foremost thing you need to do in training your dog is to be consistent. You need to establish a communication pattern for conveying what you want them to do. Border Collies aim to please, and it's very important that you teach them what to do and then duly reward them for doing a great job. Positive reinforcement works so well for these dogs because they revel in the joy of doing a good job and pleasing their trainer/owner.

An important aspect that needs to be taught early on is obedience. You never know what kind of terrain and surroundings you're going to have when on a search. Searches in busy urban areas have so many noise and movement distractions with people and cars. This can be a dangerous place to be searching. I've been in remote wooded areas, which don't have the distractions of cars and people, but once a dog sees a squirrel scurrying about, they have a natural instinct to chase it. What you have to do is train your dog to stay focused on the task at hand. Obedience is key in this situation and also if you need to stop your dog at a fraction of a seconds notice to prevent their death or injury. I train my dogs to focus on my commands while staying on task.

It takes a lot of training, but once they are able to focus, that's when they really get to work. Border Collies are born herders. They are extremely hard-working dogs, and they will work with you until you tell them to take a break. I've literally seen dogs work until they dropped from exhaustion because they were so determined and focused on the task at hand.

In order to train dogs for HRD work, you must obtain training sources/human remains This should contain bone, tissue, teeth, and anything related to human decomposition. Most of the items come from the master trainer on our team who receives the materials from a medical examiner, who is authorized to provide such materials to accredited persons. I have purchased some other items online from Skulls Unlimited, a site that specializes in osteological (bone) materials. Some friends who had their teeth pulled graciously gave them to me, and they are of great use.

These training materials are usually best kept cold to preserve them, so I store them in the freezer in my basement.

Of course, this elicits jokes from everyone who knows me, including my own family. Everyone is aware what is in the freezer. Whenever someone asks, "What are we having tonight?" someone invariably responds with something like, "Look in the freezer!"

My kids always tell each other not to come to dinner at my house because I burn everything like that hand I have in the freezer. My dogs have to be trained to smell burnt body parts, so I have a burnt hand to use in training The jokes are endless, including the one about not staying the night or you'll wind up as a cadaver for training!

Once the training materials are in place, I give the dogs a command, or trigger, to go search. Simon and Kimber know the words "FIND IT." This triggers them to find the scent. The reward for finding it is a burlap tug toy with handles on both ends, which is specifically made for training dogs. For a brief moment it's their reward, and then it's back to training. Each of my dogs has a particular way of alerting me to a scent. Kimber is more of a barker, and Simon points with his nose, then barks. Their alerts are different, even though they're both Border Collies and come from the same litter.

When working with different dogs, I have to learn when they are picking up the scent of a person/cadaver, or if they are sniffing out a critter during a long search and boredom kicks in. With Kimber, I know she's working when her tail is not moving. She has picked up a scent of a body and is focused. If I see her tail wagging while she's sniffing around, she's picked up the scent of a critter. Simon will bring me a stick if he's worked a long period of time and falls into boredom. At these times I abruptly remind them they are working and I say "get back to work" and the mind goes back to working mode.

Many times a dog will bark in excitement, but we need to learn our dogs' body language. With Kimber, I spot a brief second when the seriousness of a situation kicks in and she tries to find the source of the smell: spinning in circles, sniffing on the ground, scenting, very frantic behavior. Have you seen a dog play with a ball when suddenly the ball rolls under the couch and the dog is frantically searching under there? They display that type of behavior when they're trying to figure out the source of a scent. I let my dogs work it out in their heads. I find that interrupting them distracts them more than helps them, but every handler is different, as is every dog. Simon displays the same frantic behavior, but he sometimes gives a strange, squealing bark before he gets to the source as if to say, "It's here!"

I do the same things I do in training when we are out on a real search. I sit them down and get their attention by looking into their faces and say, "Are you ready to go to work?" When they get excited over that, I say in a loud and commanding voice, "Find it! Go find it!" And then off they go sniffing the ground and air looking for that scent that will get them their reward. Once they find it, they give me the continuous bark alert, which is called an aggressive alert.

There are different types of alerts: most of the time you will hear passive or aggressive. Some dogs aren't barkers, so their alerts are passive. Sitting or lying down is a passive alert. When Kimber first began her training as a pup, her alert was passive. She'd find something, bump it with her nose, and would sit. Barking is an aggressive alert. Most people like that, but some dogs just won't do it. Kimber started doing an aggressive alert after she saw Simon do it. Like brother, like sister. My dogs are hard workers, so their diet has to reflect the amount of protein and nutrients they need in order to effectively do their job. I do not feed them garbage food. I frequently feed them raw chicken for protein and they are given vitamins. I keep them on a grain-free food as well. This diet keeps them healthy and strong for all the hard work they have to endure.

Some dogs have died from exhaustion because their handlers didn't give them time to rest and rehydrate. You may think that it isn't a big deal for a dog to work that hard for more than fifteen or twenty minutes in the heat, but it's comparable to a human running as fast as he or she can for that same amount of time. My dogs work in all types of weather conditions. Extreme heat and cold are hard for everyone, so for me I feel it's best for me to have more than one working dog so one can rest and rehydrate while the other dog is working. Most handlers only have one and I do understand why. It's a lot of work training for hours and hours.

Dogs, whether working, sporting, or toy breeds, are an important part of our lives. They are everything from best friends to protectors to even mental health counselors. It is a proven fact that people with animals live longer and happier lives. Kimber, Kindle, and Simon are an integral part of my home. They are my buddies and friends, and we play and take walks together. They often go everywhere with me, even to the store, and wait patiently in the truck for me to come back.

They are allowed to go into some stores because they are rescue dogs, and people just love them.

Kindle gets along so well with people that the head of our search and rescue group suggested that I train her to be a live find air scent dog rather than a cadaver (HRD) dog like Kimber and Simon. It's been a challenge for me to switch my training skills to a different track. It's a bit slow going. Kindle is eight months old, but she is responding well to training. It takes a special dog to be an effective search and rescue dog, and Kindle has that fire and determination that is needed. Working dogs have such a strong work ethic and drive.

Kindle is my first live-scent dog. An air scenting dog works by finding human scent that is primarily airborne (hence the term). Once this dog finds the scent cone he or she follows the scent to its source. The dog is trained to indicate any source of human scent in a given area. This is ideal in an area of wilderness where few humans are present and one must find anyone in the area. The dog works off-lead, usually ranging a good distance away from the handler. However, the dog must always be under the handler's control via verbal commands and hand signals and must possess a strong trained alert to notify the handler of a find.

After training the other two of my own dogs to find human remains cadavers, Kindle's training definitely has kept me on my toes. Yes, there are certain aspects that are the same, such as obedience and focus, but it's a new territory for me, and I'm learning along the way with the dog. The more experience you have with training and taking your dog into the field gives you confidence. It's like the dogs and I learn together. With HRD training, I am pretty confident with taking the dogs in the field. I've been doing this for quite a while and experienced many different situations and always learning. Live scent training is something different and it has humbled me a bit. I do have the experience of handling a dog, which helps immensely, but in a situation when a person's life is at stake, your goal is to find them alive. Time is of the essence. It's a different kind of intensity than when using cadaver dogs.

Our beginning training started like this. I would go out with Kindle and a helper. My helper takes the dog on a leash and I have one of Kindle's toys. I'll tease her with it for a bit to grab her attention and then run about thirty feet away. I can't go too far because she is a puppy and has a short attention span. I will go hide behind a tree and my helper will take Kindle off her leash and say "Where did she go? Can you find her?" Those are the words I will eventually use when I take Kindle out on a search, so we want her to become familiar with those phrases from the start. Once Kindle is off the leash, she runs over to me and I play with her and lavish her with attention. I want her to be so happy that she has found me.

Later we will switch her to finding other people the same way with the victim being very happy and playful with her when she finds them. The victim must always be more fun and playful than the handler during training sessions. The dogs need to learn that they need to work when they are with the handler, and the victim's playfulness and joy reinforces the dog's job well done.

Now we have progressed to her looking for a victim. This victim still needs to be animated and fun. They reward her when she makes the find. Her alert is a very long bout of barking, saying they are here and I have located them. I have been able to see a change in her. She has really begun to show me that she understands that she is looking for LIVE human scent. She will stand on her hind legs to see if she can pick up the scent from a higher elevation.

I'm learning right along with Kindle, so it's been an adventure and new experience for us both. Thankfully, I have helped search with others who have worked with live-scent dogs, so I can use that experience and knowledge for when I'm working with Kindle.

Training. Courtesy of Gale St. John.

I hope that Kindle will eventually be able to do rubble work. We are practicing on rubble but this will all take time. She needs to learn balance on the rubble and continue training. Seems we have a long road a head. Once she's fully trained and certified she'll be able to search at disaster sites and find live people who may be buried underneath rubble due to a tornado, earthquake, or fire, etc. She will truly be a life-saving dog. Kindle has such a different personality from Simon and

Kimber. She's very outgoing, sweet, and constantly looking for my approval. Kindle is constantly underfoot, but she is the quietest dog I've ever owned. Even though Kindle is not even a year old, I've been bringing her out pretty much wherever I go, so she can get used to what life is like traveling .

People constantly ask me what it takes to be a successful search and rescue handler. My reply is always the same: train, read and learn all you can and then train more and train harder. I have learned that inexperience hinders yourself and the dog. I was once working with one of my dogs and I knew the human remains were nearby, but the dog couldn't locate the scent. I was at fault because I wasn't paying attention to the weather factors in how the scent was traveling.

It was through experience and talking with other trainers that I was able to read the weather and wind, as well as read what my dog's behavior was telling me, so that I can assess the situation, have the dog refocus, and move to a different area. I have been training for quite some time now, and I still get frustrated. I learn something new with every training exercise and every case that I work on. There's always something new to encounter, and I mark it up as knowledge to help me out the next time I'm out in the field.

It's your responsibility as a handler to make sure your dogs are in top condition when in the field. Searches are conducted in every kind of weather condition, year round. Heat and humidity can really tax a dog's system. Border Collies are so focused that I've seen dogs collapse from exhaustion and dehydration because they wouldn't give up. Dogs may only be able to work for no more than twenty minutes at a time when the temperatures are extremely hot or cold. I'll work Kimber for twenty minutes, and when that time is up, I'll get Simon and work him while Kimber drinks water and rests in the comfort of my truck.

The confidence, or lack thereof, of the trainer makes a big difference in the dog's behavior. A lot of stress in involved in being a handler for a search and rescue dog. The pressure is on you to help make the find. All eyes are on you and expecting you to do your job in order to find a missing loved one. You have the grieving family in mind and you want so badly for them to have closure, and it is very important that you keep your wits about you and not let your stress and insecurities come through. Beginners will of course be intimidated and insecure at first, but with practice and guidance from experienced trainers and handlers, confidence will build in both the trainer and the dog. But you must make sure that you don't become too confident. If you're overconfident,you're just setting yourself up for failure. Trust yourself and your dog, and when you go out there working as a team, you have a goal. Keep focused as this is important in not only looking for signs or evidence but it could be what saves you and your dogs life. The more experience and training you have, the better you'll be able to recognize things faster and see mistakes that you've made in the past and be able to correct them quicker and move on. I can think back to many times when I was out in the field and did something that to me now seems so stupid, but I didn't know any better. I definitely have learned from my mistakes, and I have become a better trainer and handler because of them. I have been lucky to have had a knowledgeable master trainer to work with from our team. It is because of her, too, that I have grown and improved as a handler .

Chapter 18

BLIND DRIVE

I never go on cases where my help is not requested or where I don't feel an urge to go. I cannot go on searches on opposite sides of the country on account of the mileage and hotel expenses. Looking back, one could say all the elements in this case conspired that I go to investigate this case in person.

It was June 2008. A little girl had gone missing in Orlando. My friend Brian, who was my partner at the time and host of his own missing persons blog, called me up and said, "Gale, we need to work on this case ASAP. Another child is missing." I didn't know anything about the case at the time. He began to tell me about the area where she went missing.

Brian does dream drawing, which means just that: he interprets his dreams through his drawings. He simply draws whatever he dreams the night before, and then tries to interpret it. Brian does not claim to be a psychic, but the information he has conveyed from his dreams has been prophetic in that it has helped me in previous cases.

He said, "I won't tell you about my dream drawing. I just want to hear what you have to say. Do a show with me on it."

I agreed. "Okay, Brian. I don't know much, but I'll jump in and tell you what I begin to see."

We began to do the Ustream show, *Missing Persons—The Psychic View*. As we talked I started seeing things. I coined the term "blind drive" many years ago. It describes a drive I do through an area just as a fishing expedition, in order to get a sense of the place. I pay attention to nothing but the pull I feel toward the missing person. I look at no street signs or anything at all that can divert my focus.

I said to Brian, "If I could do a blind drive it would make all the difference in the world because I am now seeing a few things that concern me. I feel a parent is involved in this."

Brian and I always argue on cases, which I'm not crazy about, but I think our audiences do enjoy the banter. He said, "I totally disagree with you, Gale. I dreamed it was an accident." My feelings were far different and they worried me.

I said, "Brian, what I'm seeing is a park-like setting. There's a comfort level there which makes me feel uneasy. I see certain types of flowers that would be in the area. I also see a fence, a really tall chain link fence in the area." These are some of the markers I begin to look for when I am on location and looking for the missing person.

He asked me, "What would you say if we could raise the funds to get you there? Let's put it out there!" The funds were raised in three or four days. I was in shock.

I hopped in my car with my daughter Tamra; my nineteen-year-old student, Travis, from the television show *Psychic Kids;* Carrie, a dog trainer; Mula, Carrie's white Shepherd cadaver dog; and Hilo, my Shepherd cadaver dog. Hilo was my cadaver dog before I got Kimber and Simon. After this case Hilo was placed as a protection dog. He was more suited to that situation and was happier there than doing search and rescue.

We drove nonstop for twenty hours to Florida and arrived in the Orlando area on August 10. We checked into a motel, courtesy of one of Brian's viewers who paid for our stay as her donation. Other than the donations we received from Brian's readers, we did not receive, nor would we have accepted, any money for our work on this case.

The next morning, we got up bright and early, took a look around, and decided to do the blind drive. We were led directly to the house where the little girl's family lived. There we had what I call one of those "holy moly!" moments because the media was all over: in people's yards, in trucks, in tents, and running around with microphones. We realized we had Ohio plates and didn't want the media to figure out who we were and why we were there. I didn't want any media attention.

As we drove away from the house, I said to Travis, "Okay, Travis. Let's turn it on." I began to go in the wrong direction on purpose, and he said, "I'm not feeling anything." I nodded, "That's what I'm trying to teach you, Travis," and I turned in the other direction. He began to shout, "I get it, I get it!" He got so excited when he picked up on the vibration. Tamra was filming with her video camera the entire time so all of our conversations and reactions and even off-color expletives were recorded during our blind drive.

Travis proceeded to explain to Tamra what I was trying to teach him. That feeling of "I get it!" as he put it, comes from the solar plexus. It feels like a cord pulling you hard and you can't stop it or keep yourself from moving toward wherever it is that is pulling you.

While I'm driving during a blind drive, I'm not looking at much of anything except traffic. Sometimes I've walked in front of cars when I'm conducting a blind drive on foot so I have to be careful. Tamra always looks out for me.

We kept driving down the street and I was feeling the vibrations more as the pull became stronger and stronger. When we got to the end of the street where the family lived, I turned right onto a side street and I said, "It's really feeling funny here. I'm feeling something. This is real!" Travis felt he was going to vomit and that is very common when the vibrational pull is very strong and when a missing person's body is nearby. At that point you have to shut off the emotions that are associated with the death or you'll lose the focus of your work. I was teaching my student when to shut down.

At that point I stopped the car. I can't even describe what I was feeling when I had turned onto the side street. Like Travis, I felt very sick to my stomach. I felt as if someone had punched me in the stomach and knocked all the wind out of me. I have been helping find missing persons for many years, and I know I must shut down these feelings when they happen, but this was so very strong. The body of the missing girl was very close. I called the police non-emergency number, and an officer answered for the lead detective on the case. He said, "Are you those damn psychics from Ohio?" I said, "Hello! Thanks for the warm reception!"

For all he knew I could have killed the little girl and left her there, so I said, "Why don't you come out and investigate?" He said, "Why don't you go back home and mind your own business?" I was trying to be so respectful, saying, "Yes sir," but I was losing my patience.

I swallowed hard, tried to regain some composure, and in my best telephone voice I told him, softly and slowly: "I realize this might sound crazy, but I feel we have located her. We do have two cadaver dogs that have reacted to something close by and we see a bag in the water. At the very least, could you just send someone out? I'm not saying I'm right. I'm saying at least give it a chance." He said, "We have it under control, and if you continue we're going to have you arrested." Then I heard a click.

I was very frustrated by the disrespect the officer had for me and my crew. We were led here and only wanted to help. We all stood there looking at each other, and Travis said, "What do we do next?"

We knew there was water in the area where the pull was coming from, and if we waded into that water, we might walk over the body and destroy evidence. I then pointed to something. "Look, there's a black garbage bag skimming the surface." There was also a dead snake floating in the water.

I said, "I'm going to call the regular 911 number because that will be the police instead of the county sheriff." I dialed 911 and told the dispatcher, "Listen, we need someone to come out. We've been here searching for the missing little girl and have come across something that might be significant."

Then they transferred me to another guy. He didn't give me the damn-psychics-from-Ohio spiel, but told me to get the hell out of there. "We don't need any more problems than we have," he said very curtly.

I persisted, "We are going to stay here until somebody comes out." The answer was a resounding "No. You are not."

We left the area and went back a couple of hours later to get the police to come out there. We got the exact same results: nothing.

I was disgusted. I called one of the team leaders from Equusearch, which is a search and rescue team from Texas. We have a good relationship and he trusts the work that I do, but he told me he couldn't convince anybody to come out.

Three days later, the lead detective went on television and announced there were other people from another state who were out there searching for the missing girl with dogs and that our dogs would indicate on animal remains. He said, "Stay away from them," stating Equusearch was the only real deal search and rescue team.

We were so very frustrated. We knew where the little girl's body was located, but we couldn't get anyone to look in the area we had pinpointed. We didn't want to disturb the evidence by looking ourselves. There was nothing else we could do, so we packed up and headed home.

Upon our return home, Nancy Grace's producer called me and asked me to appear on her show in regard to the case of the missing girl. I was very careful not to say anything that would give anything away to cause people to go tramping through the area where I felt the body would be discovered. Grace's producers were asking whether our dogs were simply detecting the presence of animal bones. We took the field producer and her team into a wooded area where I knew there were animal bones, and the dogs clearly did not indicate the presence of any animal bones. Cadaver dogs are trained to detect the decomposition scent of human bodies, not animals.

When the missing girl's remains were finally found and recovered in the woods off the street where the family lived, I wasn't at all surprised. We were there, I sensed it, and we all knew it. And we have the video to prove it.

I can be heard saying, "All right, I've got to pull over. Guys, I'm being really pulled there." It was the exact area where the little girl's remains were located.

I had been asking Equusearch to explore that same area for months, and once the body was found, the team leader told me, "Gale, I could kick myself!"

Before the trial even began, I was on *Issues with Jane Velez-Mitchell*. I told Jane, "Nobody's going to be happy with what I'm going to say: the mother is going to get away with it. She's going to walk." The mother who went to trial for killing her daughter was acquitted. Justice, in my opinion, was not done.

Chapter 19

LOOKING FOR GRACE

Grace, a twenty-year-old sophomore at Indiana University, disappeared in Bloomington on June 3, 2011. Eyewitnesses spotted her car in the vicinity of 11th Street and Morton Street, and also on College and 10th Street on the morning she went missing.

The girl's parents reached out to me in mid-July through Gary, a crime scene investigator who is a friend of mine. Gary and the parents requested I go out and search the area with my dogs after a massive search of Bloomington yielded no results at all.

On Sunday, July 17, I left my home for Bloomington. We arrived at the motel around 3:00 p.m. I waited for Gary to give me the go-ahead to go out and search, but he was in a meeting and I was getting antsy. That always seems to be an issue with me because I like to get started as soon as I get to my destination. I could not wait any longer and decided to head out and feel what the area decided to offer. It was truly a blind drive because at this point I had no clue as to where Grace was last seen. I knew she was a college student so I headed out to the streets surrounding the university.

As I drove through the intersection of Morton Street and 11th, I started to hear a song. My son Dustin is eighteen and a gifted composer and musician. The song I was hearing was a lovely ballad he wrote that was called, "Simple Things to Appreciate." But it wasn't Dustin's voice I heard singing the song. It was a woman's. I was hearing one lyric over and over again: *Keep going to the end of life...*

I started singing my son's ballad along with the young woman, and the singing stopped. I drove around to the intersection of College and 9th Street and she began to sing again. She sang the entire time I circled an apartment building nearby. I later found out she was last seen at a party in this building. "I am here," I said directly to her. I thought okay, you mean for me to be here. We searched until it got dark and marked down some specific areas to explore the following day. There is always a certain amount of information I will not publicly disclose because we don't need to attract attention. There is a distraught family and it serves absolutely no purpose to have a media circus involved in the investigation.

I went back to the motel confused over the feeling I had when I was in the downtown area. Obviously there could not be a body there because somebody would have seen it. But I kept thinking—why did I hear the song and why was it sung by a woman?

At this point, I really needed to go to sleep to prepare to start fresh the next day. It would be a rough outing with excessive heat warnings issued by the National Weather Service. This was dangerous, not only for my dogs but for myself.

I woke up at 4:30 a.m., got my dogs ready to go, and we were out the door and in my truck at 5:00 a.m. Don, the Bloomington coordinator of the search for Grace, would not be able to meet up with me until 3:00 in the afternoon, so I was on my own.

I hit many areas where I felt very definite sensations and vibrations, but I also sensed they were not related to Grace's disappearance. Still, I considered it a duty to check them out. I came back to the motel at around 2:00 p.m. to give the dogs and myself a rest and time to cool off.

Like clockwork, Don called and said, "Where are you right now?" I told him I was back at the motel. He said, "I will be there in five, so be ready and in the truck with Simon and Kimber." I met Don in the parking lot and he hopped in my truck and we drove off. He said, "Where are the areas you feel I need to see with you?" I told him where I had picked up something, but explained I also felt some things totally unrelated to this case. He sort of chuckled.

We stopped at one of the areas I mentioned and I said, "Look over there, Don. I feel deep sadness, but it's not connected to Grace." Don said, "I know why. Last week a woman was stabbed to death and her purse was discovered in that area two days ago."

We went to another area that interested him. We did a search, found nothing, and moved on to another spot. I said, "Don, I feel a deep sadness emanating from this location, but again, I do not feel it is related to Grace at all." He said,

"Wow, you are correct again! A short time ago a young girl was murdered and this is where her body was found." Good grief! That was two murders in such a small area and short time period.

Don said, "Let me take you somewhere else now." We drove on, arrived at the spot, and he said he felt something suspicious. It was the spot where I first got stuck in circles and I didn't know why. It is an area with apartment buildings. It's located near the university so the tenants of the buildings are mainly students, so the buildings are typical for student housing: not upscale, but not a rough part of town either.

I told Don that I kept on circling the area and knew it could not be because there was a body somewhere, since there are no woods or grassy spots to hide a body. All other areas would be too visible for a body to not be discovered.

I parked the truck and we brought out the dogs. I brought out Kimber first since I know she paces herself well, but she had been working for twelve hours. I held her head and looked in her eyes and said, "Kimber, look at Momma. Let's do this one more time for Momma. Let's go find her."

She looked at me as if to say, "I can do this, Mom. Let's go." She puffed out her chest and began to prance around, as if proud of herself. She realized I trusted her. Dogs pick up our feelings so well and in turn externalize them in their gait. I pointed out things for her to check as we meandered up and down an alley and through a parking lot.

We came upon a tall hedge of grass, and I saw Kimber perk up like a fresh dog, full of energy. She was thrilled! She's on it, she's on the scent! She stuck her head in the tall grass and her excitement even woke me up. I was so dead tired by then I thought I was going to fall on my face from exhaustion.

I said, "Shh, Don. Quiet!" There was a little patch of grass by a tree and Kimber moved over to that and buried her head in it. I can tell when she's found something because her whole body language changes.

I watched her put her nose to the ground, stop, and pause. I looked into her eyes and could see her wheels turning, her nose waiting for the wind. Then there was a teeny bit of breeze and she stuck her nose way up into the air. Sniff, sniff, her tail went straight up, and she was moving.

There was a fenced-in area in an alley that contained a dumpster. Kimber ran to the gate of the fence and tried to get her body through a hole in it where the fencing was broken. She got stuck so I got her out and flipped open the little gate in the fence. She then ran and plastered herself against the wall of the concrete building to try and get a scent. At this point I don't say anything. I want the dogs to work this out in their minds.

Kimber got on her tippie toes, bumped the lid off the dumpster, and began to bark and indicate. She went in front of the dumpster and stood on her hind legs. Then she ran back behind the dumpster and indicated again. I rewarded her with her toy and we went back to the truck to see what Simon could sniff out.

Simon is very vocal before he even gets to the source. He is very animated and clear on what he wants and what he smells. Kimber is quiet and methodical in the way she works. I can see her body language change but she will not be vocal until she finds the actual source of the scent. I said to Don, "I don't want Simon to follow the same path. I want to wait to see what he does."

I brought out Simon at a different angle and had him on a twenty-foot lead. All of a sudden he got up to the grass, buried his head in it, just like Kimber, and he got really excited. He did the same thing Kimber did; his nose went up in the air and then back down, and then he ran to the dumpster area and squealed. He was frantically digging with his paws trying to get through the fence. He was digging and pawing and scratching, running over to the door to the fence, and then he got his head stuck in the hole. I pulled him out, flipped open the gate, and he ran in there. I never saw that nose move so fast, sniffing in circles and looking like a mental case.

Simon went to a source behind the dumpster and started barking and barking and bumping and bumping. That is what they do. And by that time Don and I were thinking, by God, we've got something! We worked all day, only to come out of those woods with two very disappointed dogs.

We went on, and drove through the city area around nine o'clock at night. From there, we called Gary and told him what had happened. He said, "You better get a hold of the mom and dad."

We had a short meeting with the parents. They are a handsome couple, well put together except for the visible ravages of the strain and the pain from their daughter's disappearance. They wanted to go out there with the dogs.

We parked in a different place when we went back to the location with the parents, which is a bad way to bring in the dogs because the wind was blowing in the other direction. I explained, "This is what's going to happen. They're going to pass the area and then they're going to turn around."

I brought Kimber around, and all of a sudden she did the thing she is famous for. She put the brakes on as if to say, "Wait a minute, what is that?" Then she spun around, nose to the ground, went to the dumpster area, and hit it as hard as she could, barking and bumping. I brought Simon out and we had an exact repeat. He passed the area and then he went back, barking and bumping.

The parents said they wanted to bring in a certified dog to verify this. I had told everybody from the start that although my dogs and I had completed and fully met all of the criteria for certification, the actual piece of paper would not arrive until October 2011, which was in three months.

At that point, the girl's parents were not able to get anyone, so I drove back home. The dogs and I were exhausted from the heat and the toll the investigation took out of all of us.

That night, Monday, July 18, I was scheduled to appear on the Internet radio show, *Cubanarama Missing N America*, hosted by my dear friend Marta Sosa, to talk about our search. After the program aired, I got a call from Gary. He had a message from the girl's parents. They did not want me there any longer and I was not to return to the area because they were upset that I had discussed the case on the radio. I was not aware that the parents didn't want me to talk about the investigations with others. I feel that the more people who know about a case the better because you can have many extra pairs of eyes and ears open. It is a good and ethical thing to explain the rules before the investigation instead of telling you afterward, through a third party, that you broke them.

I became very upset, then very angry, and ultimately very sad that I was not able to continue the investigation. However, after I got some physical and mental rest from the entire ordeal, I calmed down and came to one conclusion: this is where I had to be, and let the rest follow its course.

On Tuesday, July 19, I got another call from Gary. He said the girl's parents went to the police department, told them my dogs had indicated over a particular area, and wanted to get it verified. The officers told them you can go ahead and have a private dog do a search, but we already know about the dumpster and the landfill. We had a police cadaver dog indicate in that area. There was their verification. The landfill now had to be searched, and Grace is in all likelihood gone.

I am not broken and neither are my dogs. I have the faith to keep on going. I understand the parents' reaction to my search and to the further confirmation of our findings during the radio program. For them, it meant the end.

The entire month and a half their daughter was missing, Grace's parents were paralyzed by hope, moving every which way, but really not moving at all. Now they had to sit still and eventually move forward, but perhaps not in the direction they wanted to go. They still have hope. I hope they find some solace, and can at least bring Grace home.

In April 2012, I was asked by some local residents to go back to Bloomington to search for Grace, and I didn't hesitate when accepting the search. This is one of those cases I can't shake, like Jimmy and the Hartman kids. It's when you know you're so damn close it could bite you, and I knew I wouldn't feel at ease until I found Grace.

I headed to the college town with my daughter Tamra and my two faithful companions, Kimber and Simon. People who were familiar with the case had suggested we search in a couple of areas I had never ventured into during the initial search. I found absolutely nothing of interest there so we left and went back to the area of the railroad tracks outside of town. It is a very dangerous area because there is no way to get off the rails because there isn't much of a shoulder on either side of the track, and there is a very steep incline from the track to the ditch below. We decided to approach the area near the tracks from a different direction and found a little area of clay ground. The area had received a heavy rain the night before, which is great for the dogs, but not for walking. Tamra slid, fell on her butt, and slid all the way down to the bottom of the ditch. Kimber gave me a little jerk, slid down in the mud, and I went down with her. Now I had a muddy dog, muddy hair, a muddy daughter, and we looked like we were doing army maneuvers. Tamra and I had a big fight, like typical mother and daughter. We walked out of this wooded area near the tracks and on to this street with people going about their way, and we were arguing and looking like mud monsters. I'm sure the people on the sidewalk looked at us perhaps thinking it was finally the zombie invasion.

Tamra and I decided we needed to go back to the motel and get ourselves cleaned up. While we were back there I called Gary to let him know I was in town to investigate, and I wanted to go over some things with him. I asked him, "Remember the first time I was out in an area and I got stuck?" He said he did. I had snapped a picture of the area where Tamra and I had just been and sent it to his cell phone. I said, "Gary, I'm going to put this to you. All I know is that the first time I went driving around, I didn't know where I was, and it grabbed me. When I went back, it grabbed me again. I feel a comfort level about the person she was with so I'm not thinking it's a stranger type of abduction. I could be wrong, but I am not feeling panic. I feel that this person ditched her so quickly he was able to establish an alibi, and what bothers me is the people who have already been questioned by the police." Gary said, "Gale, I think you're really close to something." Even though we had a very strong lead we knew we had to take our time and not run into it like a bull in a china shop. Grace had been missing for almost a year, so we're going to be looking for bones. Gary asked me what the terrain was. I said, "We're going to need a couple of hikers or rock climbers. This is a terrain like no other and hard to traverse, especially for the dogs and for me with my bad knees."

Gary told me he had been to a conference about the Green River Killer, a serial killer from Washington state who had been convicted for murdering forty-eight women. I asked him what the Green River Killer had to do with Grace's case. He talked about how the serial killer lowered his victims down steep inclines so the bodies were not found. I said, "Gary, this dropoff could be the undoing of the case if we can't go there. I can give hikers or rock climbers a quick class and show them how to work the dogs and I can command the dogs, but we have to be very careful because the guard rail is only one foot away from the road. We could be in a lot of danger. We have to go on the other side and try to go up. And if that body is there, the vegetation would be as tall as me. That body would have never been found." If her body was taken to that location around June, conditions would be about the same. When Tamra and I were at the location earlier in the day, I lit a cigarette—even though I don't smoke—to see what the scent might be doing in that area. I realized the smoke first collected under the cool greenery, and then it went up into the trees, so I knew I wasn't getting a vibration that originated on the highway. Nobody, not even the dogs, would have picked up the scent if the body was located along the steep incline. Gary and I knew that the only way to explore this area is to climb it, and it will be no easy task.

Gary and I are formulating a plan to go to the area in the summer and enlist the help of volunteers who are skilled at climbing over treacherous terrain. We're going to have to break the area down piece by piece, and it could take months in order to search the entire area. I am hellbent on conducting this search. I wake up in the middle of the night thinking about it. It's almost like I can't work on another case until I complete this mission for Grace.

Gary asked me, "What are you going to do if we find her?"

I told him, "I'm going to slap you on the back and say, 'Go to it, old man. Deal with the media!'" My main concern is that Grace is finally found and her family is finally at peace.

— Chapter 20 —

THE EYES OF TEXAS

As with any occupation, there are projects or aspects of the job that are frustrating or rewarding. One case stands out as the most rewarding of all my cases to date.

I had been asked by a search group to travel to Texas to help them find a teenager who had disappeared two years earlier. The group was one of the most experienced groups of searchers with whom I had ever worked. They marked every area they searched on a map and forwarded it to the local law enforcement. The group was excellent at searching but not very consistent on how they worked. They would jump all over the county and search in separate areas rather than cover an entire area before moving onto another section. I had talked to one of the searchers on the phone and gave them some information as to where the girl would be found, but nothing turned up. After two years of fruitless searching, they called to ask if I would be willing to travel to Texas to help search in person. The search team rallied for support and was able to collect donations to cover my gas and hotel expenses. My upcoming visit was even covered by the local online news source. Needless to say, a lot of hope was riding on my visit to Texas.

Gary was also invited to participate in the investigation. Tamra usually accompanies me on investigations as well, but she had just started a new job and wasn't able to come along. My son Dustin, who is a musician, was nineteen and unemployed at the time. I said to him, "You know what? You've never been much outside of Toledo, Ohio, so you're going to Texas. And if you're going to do it right, you're going out the first time with the rattlesnakes." Little did we know what dreadful self-fulfilling prophecy I had just uttered.

Dustin and I traveled down to Texas, and Gary met us there. The very first thing we did was have a meeting with the local law enforcement and called a press conference with the media. Our goal was to get everything out of the way at once so that Gary and I could do our work without being hampered by the local authority or media. The local police department actually said they appreciated we were there to help. It was such a good experience because the law enforcement was open to anything, which is not always the case.

The search started out with a blind drive. I began the search at Caroline's house, which is where she had last been seen. I could feel her alive in certain places. I could feel there were some places where she liked to play. I got to a parking lot on the side of a motel and I could feel she was on the trail walking, and then I lost her. She could have been picked up from that trail or area. I picked up something strange in another area and kept going in circles. Dustin said, "Mom, you've been going around in circles." I said, "I know, I'm stuck." I decided to shut down the blind drive and try and clear my head. I couldn't figure out why I was stuck. I felt something strange that kept me going around in circles. It might have been part of the route the kidnappers took before they dumped the body. I feel that Caroline's disappearance was foul play, and being that I didn't feel a sense of panic, I think the perpetrator was somebody she knew. In cases where a stranger has abducted the victim, I feel a great sense of fear at the last place I sense they were.

At this point, someone in the search group said, "We need to come back to town because we have approval from Caroline's mother's cousin, who is now living in the house, to bring the dogs inside the house." Caroline's mother was living in another city at the time, but I was able to speak with her and asked if her mother's instincts were kicking in as to where Caroline might be. I told her to meditate on it and let me know if she saw, felt, or sensed anything. She did get back to me and named some areas where she felt her daughter might be. What Caroline's mother said confirmed what I had felt at first, and I marked the locations, which were areas I had visited on the second half of my blind drive. Most areas that I was picking up on had not been searched at that time because Gary and I were focused on taking the search back to the beginning and going about it in a true search mode where areas are divided into grids and every area of a grid is searched before continuing onto the next. There was a lot of difficult terrain in these search areas. Some were filled with cacti, others with deep gullies. The weather was about 102 degrees, humid, and direct, scorching sun. We could only work so many minutes in that kind of heat so we would work one dog on a thirty-two-inch lead for twenty-five minutes and then work the other dog while the first one rehydrated and rested.

Now here comes the self-fulfilling prophecy of what I told Dustin before our trip. We did encounter a rattlesnake up close and personal. I must have stepped on the snake not knowing it was there, and I thought I heard something, but I was focused on what my dog Simon was doing. When I sent him back in another direction, I turned around and I saw the snake there. Simon came running up, and I called him to a down position. "Down!" I said, almost in a whisper. "Down, down, Simon!" He obeyed. Another girl started walking up and I said, "Don't move, April. Don't anybody move." The snake kind of coiled like it was going to strike and all of a sudden it slithered off and away from us and we got out of there.

After our snake adventure, we went to search the actual house. I took Kimber, who is my go-to dog on a house search because she slows herself down and paces herself in a building or a house. Simon is the bull in the china shop. We went in and Kimber searched the hardwood floors and the carpet in every room in the house. At one point Kimber showed some heavy interest but no indication, meaning there was no cadaver in the house, so obviously we thought any harm to Caroline might not have happened here.

In March 2013, a local man discovered Caroline's remains near a lake ten miles away from her hometown. She was discovered in an area that I had picked up on, but we weren't able to search due to time constraints and the oppressive heat. The general location had been added to my GPS and was one of the areas we were going to search when we went back to the area. The Colorado City Police Department was fantastic to work with, and I don't have any doubt that they will be able to obtain evidence of what happened and bring justice to Caroline.

Chapter 21 —————

THE COCKY KILLER

Sometimes it can be very hard to avoid learning any background information about a case, especially when the story is plastered all over the news. It was very hard to avoid knowing about a young woman's disappearance due to the massive amount of media coverage that surrounded her case and most notably, her husband's cocky and arrogant willingness to appear on many television and radio programs regarding his wife's disappearance and frankness about his prior marriages. This missing woman was his fourth wife, and his third wife had died under very suspicious circumstances. It also didn't help that the husband was the former police sergeant of their suburban Chicago community.

I went to the Chicago area with my friend Jim, the private investigator who was hired to help find the missing woman. I brought along my dogs to see if they could pick up anything once we arrived at a location where she might be found. We started with a blind drive and decided that we'd begin from their house. It was so eerie because her car was still sitting in the driveway. I couldn't pick up that she was alive, and I had heard gunfire. I knew she was dead when she left the house. The home is located in a typical suburban subdivision with winding streets that go nowhere. Jim stated that he had been to the house many times but always got lost due to the winding streets. I didn't have any problem finding my way around because I sensed the husband's routine in getting out of there.

Jim said, "I'm going to take you to a site where we have unofficial permission to go." I knew it was a place where the husband was very comfortable, where he carried out certain activities that might be considered related to what I sensed happened to the woman. The dogs showed no interest at the first location. We went to another location nearby and Kimber showed a marked interest by pawing at the ground. I led her away from the area and we approached it from another direction. Again she pawed the ground in the same location. I immediately took her back to the truck and retrieved Simon to see if he could pick up anything. I did not want to give him any clues as to where we had been so I released him to see what he could sense. He smelled other spots, such as where I shuffled my feet or where Kimber had been, and then he went to the same spot and pawed the ground, just as Kimber had done. We knew we had something at this location. We are now doing more mapping and returning to the area, so we are getting somewhere. There is another area I want to check out that may lead us to some definite clues. The woman's body has not been recovered, and her husband is currently in prison for the death of his third wife. Even though her husband is behind bars and can't harm anyone else, I do want her body to be found so that her family and friends can finally receive closure.

Chapter 22

DISASTER PREPAREDNESS

I have been able to sense natural disasters from a very young age. From ages seven to about ten, I would have visions of areas that had been hit by something and left a path of total destruction. I started to write about the visions of disasters I saw shortly after I started seeing them. One afternoon, I had just gotten home from school and the entire living room went dark. I said to myself, "Here we go again!" This vision happened in the 1970s, but it looked like what we would call a flat screen television today and it appeared in front of me. It was like the whole world opened up to me on a screen. I could hear talking and see what the people were doing. I saw ordinary people, and then it was as if they were showing a video of a tornado on television. I finally verbalized, "What does all this mean?" I heard someone, as if he or she were standing next to me, say, "You're going to see tornadoes where tornadoes don't usually happen. All kinds of things that don't normally happen, but they will happen."

The room became light again and I wondered what the hell is going on? If what my spirit guide or whoever said is true, I don't want to know it! Storms where there were never storms, active volcanoes where they weren't any. It didn't make sense. One of the things I was told was that Japan would be hit by a major earthquake and people would be sick from their own materials. I couldn't understand what this meant at the time, but now I do.

The visions stopped when I was ten, but from then on, I get a terrible feeling when a natural disaster is going to strike. A lot of people have these nagging feelings about not going somewhere and they don't heed them. Perhaps we all should.

Cadaver dogs are not trained just once and are good to go. I have to keep up my dogs' training so they can become better at what they do and always be at the top of their game. I work with my dogs a lot on my own and conduct training exercises with both Kimber and Simon. Dogs who have taken classes are given a public safety identification number (PS ID) through the state to acknowledge they have completed that course of training. As your dog progresses through training, you can test for pre-credentials in order to see if it is ready to take the credential test, as well as what areas your dog may need to improve on.

On March 2, 2012, Kimber and I left for Camp Atterbury, a military camp near Indianapolis, to do some search and rescue training. Everyone else who was attending the training session was coming from the north, but as I was pulling out of my driveway I saw it flash in my mind: tornadoes. I had the most uncomfortable feeling of dread. I had been terribly excited all week about going to the training exercise, but once I had the tornado warning flash through my mind, I could hardly force myself to go. It was such a nagging, ominous feeling. I kept telling myself, "Look this is stupid. Put yourself together and smile and be happy! Forget that thought. Put it out of your head!" I loaded Kimber into my vehicle and we headed to the highway. The members of the rest of the group were going to call me when they hit the one-mile point from the highway ramp so we could all arrive at the camp together. I got there an hour early so I sat in the car and listened to the radio, with Kimber secured in the seat next to me with a seatbelt, to wait until I heard from the rest of the training crew. There was a steady rain, but nothing too threatening or severe. All of a sudden, Kimber started to go crazy. I said to her, "What's the matter, baby? It's only rain." I offered her a treat, but she wouldn't have any of it, which is odd because she loves her treats.

That sinking feeling came back to me. I flipped through the stations until I landed on a weather report. A very bad storm was headed directly toward us. It suddenly became very dark, which is very unnerving when it's 2:00 p.m., and the sky turned green. Kimber was shaking and was trying to go down on the floor to hide. I realized that's why the poor thing was shaking; she could feel the atmospheric pressure changes. Dime-size hail started pounding down on my truck and I immediately started to look for a safer place to sit out the storm. I was sitting on the shoulder of the entrance ramp to the highway so I couldn't back up. I looked around to see if there was a lower spot and parked my truck under the underpass to wait out the storm. I looked at the radar on my smartphone and thought the weather system might pass quickly due to its size and speed. I called my trainer and said, "Listen, don't hurry getting down here" and explained what was happening. The hail came down for seven or eight minutes before it finally passed. The sun came out after the dark clouds moved on and I started feeling relieved. The next thing I knew the rest of my training crew were calling and were a mile away from the ramp. Kimber was exhausted from the storm and settled down to take a nap. We were about thirty minutes from Indianapolis when I called the instructor in the front vehicle. I said, "Listen, I have the weather radio on again." She said, "Are you panicking?" I said "Yes, I am panicking. I'm looking at the radar and it looks like the storm is going to move right across the highway and we're going to run into it in about seven to ten miles. It looks bad." The team members in the other vehicles were calling each other to update on what was in store for us a few miles down the road. The storm hit with a vengeance. It was raining so hard and the windshield wipers were going as fast as they could and it made no difference. We were going 10 miles per hour and I could not see what was in front of me. The light poles were bent over from the strong winds, several cars were strewn around the road and had slammed into other cars or the guard rails. We finally made it to the camp, which had not been damaged by the storm, and were immediately

told about the tornadoes that hit the nearby cities of Henrys-
ville and Marysville. Their deadly force completely leveled the
cities and surrounding areas. I totally understood my feelings
of dread in regard to this trip. I had been looking forward to
the training event all week, and then I suddenly didn't want
to leave earlier that morning. Kimber and I, not to mention
the other training team members, could have all been killed in
that storm. We were on standby during our classes and were
ready just in case our help was needed during rescue efforts.
We didn't have to lend a hand, but our training practices that
weekend seemed to resonate with us more than usual because
we knew how important the skills our dogs were learning
were to rescue efforts, especially considering crews were very
active not too far away. The specific areas of training the dogs
we were focusing on that weekend were agility and simulated search. Agility training lessens the dog's fear of walking
on unstable surfaces, such as a home that has been hit by a
tornado. A floating bridge is used in the training practices in
order for the dog to feel comfortable on a surface that isn't
steady. The dogs are also trained to go down tunnels in boxes.
The easiest way to describe this is to imagine a dog was in a
bucket being lowered into a well. This is a difficult exercise
for rescue dogs to master because they can see less in the dark
than we can. Kimber is not at an advanced level when it comes
to this type of rescue training so she was afraid.

Simulated search training involves the trainer placing a
cadaver in the woods and the dogs and handlers have to find
it. Kimber does fantastically well on simulated trainings but

no dog is ever 100 percent accurate. The human and the dogs are partners, and the handler has to have enough knowledge about scents and how to problem-solve when trying to determine if there are other factors that could prohibit the dog from picking up on the scent. Kimber and I got stuck during this training session. We were in the woods about fifteen to twenty feet away from where the cadaver items were placed. The winds were swirling and seemed to be coming from every direction. She was getting frustrated, I was getting frustrated, and I asked one of the instructors what was going on. What I learned from that experience was heat rises and cool air falls so a scent goes up and down accordingly. Humidity, barometric pressure, time of day, and whether the sun is out are all factors to how scent can be carried. When the wind is throwing the scent around and the dog can't pick up on the direct location of the scent, we have to think about all these factors and conditions, read the dog's body language, and try to help our dog locate the source by determining where the scent is coming from and move the dog over to that area in hopes they will be able to pick up the scent and locate the source. I would have used my baby powder technique, but the instructor brought out a propane device with a unit on it that produced smoke. The purpose of the exercise is to see which way the smoke is going so we can see how the wind can move the scent around the area of the cadaver's actual location. In this case the smoke went up over the tree, down again, and over the area where Kimber was stuck. It was clinging to everything.

Once I saw the smoke I had an "Aha!" experience because I was able to physically see how scent travels. Exercises like this really help with problem solving. I am grateful I learned this because it is knowledge I can hang onto and use in all situations, from searching for land cadavers to disaster work.

Chapter 23

OPPORTUNITY, MOTIVE, AND VICTIMOLOGY

Homicide detectives and profilers carefully study three elements when trying to solve a crime: opportunity, motive, and victimology. They look at suspects who had motive and opportunity to commit the crime and they examine the victimology, or crime scene, to come up with a particular method of operation or signature the killer leaves behind. I also use this criteria to explain the circumstances under which I can go and search for a missing person who is presumed dead.

Opportunity

This involves a few different variables. The first is how far the search area is from me. If the case is nearby, it's not a problem for me to conduct the search since the travel time and cost are very minimal. For the case in Japan, I would have never been able to afford the airfare, let alone the stay, without the help from the television stations. With other cases, I am enabled to conduct the search by volunteers who pay for our motel stay and our gas, which helps alleviate my out-of-pocket expenses.

The time of year and climate are also variables that fall under opportunity. I live in the Midwest, and I've had to deal with scorching heat, snowstorms, and tornadoes during investigations. There are days where it's just not viable to be searching. I have to keep the safety and health of myself, my team, and my dogs in mind.

Motivation

Some of the cases I have been involved with are spurred on by a motivation that comes from within me. It's a hard thing to explain, but it's like knowing your phone is going to ring before it does. I have a very strong, innate feeling about this person, and I feel almost physically drawn to the case. When I know there is going to be evidence, I also know it is important for me to be there. During Jimmy's case, I was hearing things so clearly I felt he was right there and I was missing something. I feel like that with Grace's case. I know it is right there under my nose, like somewhere they missed her during the original search, and I won't rest until she is found.

Victimology

In some cases, motive and victimology are inextricable. The connections are so similar it is almost like the same path. I can separate them better in murder cases when the body has already been found. It seems like there is not the same kind of push or drive if the body is still missing. The drive is to find the killer, who thinks he's gotten away with it. I feel less urgency when the body is found. In most murder cases, I don't personally look for the killer, I give information to the investigators: what the person might have been driving, where they may live, what they look like, where they may have killed the victim. The information I pass along to the investigators will hopefully help point them in the right direction to find the killer.

I once passed along information in a case, and it happened to be the same information a seven-year-old witness to the crime gave in a statement. This was further proof that what the witness said was true and that the police should follow the lead given in that information.

Sometimes it takes years to find a solution to the case. Just because we are psychic it doesn't mean there is going to be a tidy solution of loose ends in an hour, as on television. Information that is brought forward may not make sense until later on. It is almost like playing a video game and one can win the entire game. You are playing a game against a killer, and I don't like losing.

Chapter 24

POLISHING THE GIFT

Just like the dog training, I believe that people have to keep exercising their faculties or they lose them. I am continually practicing my psychic abilities so that I can pick up on vibrations and senses when I am conducting searches.

No one can be taught to be psychic, but I teach psychic development skills because I believe we all have this sense. Why? Let's take a look at animals in the wild. They know through heightened senses, feelings, and intuition when they are being preyed upon. They react with a fight or flight response.

Humans display a variety of psychic senses through many things. Children are more open to the world around them and often mention an imaginary friend. That friend may be a spirit rather than a figment of their imagination. I always tell parents to not discourage their children when they mention an imaginary friend.

Women's intuition is something that is commonly mentioned. This may be due to their motherly instincts in regard to protecting their children. Their internal radar is always on high alert to recognize when someone's watching us, to know when not to trust someone. Animals know it, we know it. If we would give this gift the time and nurturing to understand how our brain works, rather than suppress it, we could understand how it works in our favor.

How can you tell if you have psychic abilities? Some people just have hunches or feelings. If you feel like something is going to happen and a couple of days later it does happen, you have a little bit of psychic awareness. For most people it's in the moment that they realize they are clairvoyant. Second gear is knowing things a day or two ahead or you know what someone is going to say before they say it. By the time you're hearing voices—and I don't mean schizophrenic voices, I mean your spirit guides and spirits from the other side—you're in third gear. At that point you might as well take the car and go for a spin because there is no point in denying your abilities.

I went through a stage of denial with my abilities because society puts all these constraints on us and we don't want to be shunned. Sometimes when you try to walk away, it becomes stronger. After a while, one doesn't have to worry about fitting in with what society says is normal. It's much more enjoyable to live one's life and embrace all aspects of life without trying to shut it off.

There is a responsibility that comes with psychic abilities. Just because you know something is going to happen, it doesn't mean you should or have the right to say it. Some knowledge is only for me to know and nobody else. I often do not share what I know with others. Sometimes I just look, grin, and walk away. People need to figure some things out on their own, and if they receive a heads-up on the situation, they may focus too much on the situation and not the experience surrounding the situation that makes it important.

Being a psychic medium sometimes makes for a lonely existence. When you pick up on more things and know what is going to happen, it's very easy to feel isolated, especially if we are treated as an outcast. We're not going to be happy with people who don't understand what we do. We can be angry but it doesn't mean we should send out those thoughts. I try to teach my students that thoughts are things, like attracts like, so always be careful what you think because putting a thought out there creates a vibration. It's a responsibility.

Psychic ability is just like any other skill. We have to exercise it and be willing to use it so we don't lose the ability to pick up information through our psychic senses. One of the first steps you have to take is to accept and embrace your abilities. Many who are psychic fight against and ignore the messages that come through. It could be due to fear or a defense mechanism. You must accept what has been granted to you, and you will be so much happier and healthier if you live in harmony with yourself.

When I start working with a student, I begin with determining how they receive information; whether they see, hear, sense, smell, taste, or know. I work very differently with someone who primarily hears things than with someone who sees things. Maybe the student is getting one part of the message, so I work with them toward seeing things as well as hearing them. I also take them into meditation sessions to help them be able to visualize. For those who see, I know what they are seeing because I am seeing it as well, so I work with them on how they can also hear the message. But I don't push my students beyond what they can do. I want to nurture what my student has and for him or her to embrace that, but I will also work with them to see if they can strengthen other forms of psychic communication. These skills can be honed and developed if someone wants to commit to the study and put in the effort, and I think the study is up to the individual. Some people are very quick to pick up things and others struggle. There is that line. I don't understand math for the life of me, and I was able to understand it better when I helped my son with his homework, but I'm not ready to move on to calculus. My brain cannot go there. I sometimes have to help people past a struggle, but I can't make someone have something they don't have. I can't guarantee you're going to come in and be one of my students and excel in a particular area, but hopefully I can help you determine in what area you are more inclined to receive information and help you start to develop and increase that ability. I like to keep it real and fun so I take students back to when their ability first started surfacing, around the age of four years old.

My daughter Tamra and my granddaughter Alexis have psychic abilities, and now they work with me from time to time. Both of them started to mention their abilities when they were about nine or ten years old. I would be talking about a case and they would jump in and say I see this or that. I knew they were telling the truth because I received the information, so I let them chime in and encouraged them to give their input to the cases. Tamra would have more feelings about things that she couldn't explain. Alexis is now sixteen and does meditation to try to work with her own abilities.

My student, Travis, has psychic abilities to a heightened degree. When I first met him on the set of the television show *Psychic Kids*, I was able to pick up the fact that he was seeing more than the other youngsters. He was able to see and hear a lot as well as pick up empathically, and I've worked with him so he can hone his abilities and be able to relay the messages that he received. I knew we had met for a reason so I could offer him some guidance. I asked him what he wanted to do with his psychic ability, and sure enough, he wanted to help with missing person cases. He was eighteen when we started to work together, and he is now twenty-two and off doing his own thing in the psychic world.

Chapter 25

THE RELUCTANT HEIRESS

My daughter Tamra has struggled with accepting her psychic abilities and underplays what abilities she has, but in the years since she started accompanying me on cases, she has come into her own and become a great source of strength and support to me.

For the most part, Tamra knew of her psychic abilities from a young age. She didn't start doing anything with them until she was between fifteen and seventeen. At that time, she didn't know what she wanted to do with her life, and I am not certain that she does now, but when I started searching for missing persons, she started to realize what she could do with her abilities and her life. She began to go on cases with me, and she is now an enormous help. Sometimes she sees things I do not see, picks up on other details I might have overlooked, or tunes into tidbits from conversations I might not have picked up on because I was too focused on what I sensed and saw.

The first case she went on was Jimmy's. It was a very memorable case because it was her first case, the extreme cold weather conditions, and Jimmy is a spirit who has pitched in during cases and helped me pick up on clues and important details. "I remember just freezing!" she now laughs, recalling the case. "I don't recall feeling anything [in regard to what she tuned into psychically on the case], I just wanted to go on a search. I didn't know if my personal life jelled with the psychic stuff."

Apparently, something was jelling because she has been accompanying me on cases ever since. She now recalls, "The more we got involved in missing persons cases and the more research we did, the more I developed intuition. Most of the time I keep stuff to myself to try to keep a level head. I've been doing it for eight years now."

A student of mine recently laughed at one of Tamra's typical reactions during one of our investigations. He said, "Ol' Tamra, here she goes again. First she says, 'I don't want to hear about this psychic stuff,' and then she turns around and blurts, 'I have a feeling about this!'" All three of us laughed because it was true. If you want to know someone's business, just ask Tamra. She's always right and very observant to physical evidence, as well as psychic evidence. For instance, while I am talking to relatives of a missing person or having one of my dogs search the area, Tamra is observing people's postures and demeanors and looking at clues that might have been left behind. This helps me a lot in determining clues and people's attitudes that may belie some complicity or culpability.

We work very well together because Tamra clarifies things I already feel. "I think things go better because there is more energy there," she says. "I think my mom kind of picks up my energy. She's very low key, whereas I'm very hyper and always running my mouth," she laughs. "I pick up on bits and pieces, and I report on these things I say to my mom." Our energies work very well together, perhaps because we are so in synch with each other and our abilities. Her energy and encouragement lifts me up and helps me continue on.

I asked her when she felt the most about a case, in terms of everything pointing to a conclusion or resolution. "I think I did during the Florida case," she responded quickly, as if she did not have to think about this at all. "A lot of personal things were going on in my life, along with the unnecessary drama that went on with that case. I remember thinking when we were doing that video that it was very funny everyone came to the same conclusion, that they were very close. I had an intuition that they were right. It's the only time I have felt a hundred percent."

We recently drove to Maine to a family wedding. We made a stop in Salem, Massachusetts, to see some of the local tourist attractions. It is a beautiful city on the water, which still holds and treasures the legacy of the witchcraft trials as a commercial commodity. Not that there aren't bona fide historians and reputable seers in its midst, but Tamra thought it was all malarkey. She thought all of the Harry Potter paraphernalia was "cute," but she doesn't believe in any of what she calls "witch stuff," although by now she knows that Mom *knows* and *sees* things, and so does *she*.

Even though Tamra has a gift which has helped me tremendously during investigations, I don't believe that this is her life path. She goes on current cases as much as she can, but she took a two year break from missing persons investigations. "During those two years, I was kind of lost. But I loved missing persons, if not for the psychic side of it, for the families. It is something I can give back to my community, and I have been raised that way. I try to find that balance between missing persons and my own personal growth," she says.

When asked about her future, Tamra said she wants to go into something along the lines of mental health work. She is a very private person who doesn't want to put herself out there. She will definitely use her ability, but she wants to keep a lower and more private profile. When I dared to ask her what she thinks about what I do, her laughing response was, "I think you're crazy! You know, I used to be very quiet about it. If anybody asked what my parents did for a living, what could I say? 'My mom talks to dead people?' It used to terrify me, but now I'm comfortable with it. It's a part of my life that's not going to go away. I don't want to hide it anymore."

Tamra and I have a good relationship. Our whole family is very close, and although we tend to get very sarcastic with one another, bantering back and forth all the time, there is a lot of love, honor, and respect among us. "It's a comfort level," interjects my daughter. "I would never disrespect my mom; she is my parent. I won't cross that line." She is a good girl, my Tamra.

Chapter 26

THE PSYCHIC JUGGLER

I am not about to take up another trade more apt for Vegas than the fields and woods I traipse through on my searches. It's when I get home that my balancing act begins.

I have four children, and I was working on cases before any of them came along. I thankfully went into labor with my fourth child just as I'd wrapped up one case. Being a mom and a search and rescue psychic investigator is a very difficult balancing act. It's also something others have a hard time understanding. I have had neighbors ask me, "Why do you have so many people at your house all the time?" At the time I was living in a newer middle-class neighborhood. Some of the neighbors were families with young kids, and some were older and retired from working. I think my neighbors thought I was a prostitute or sold drugs with all the people coming and going at all hours of the day. I didn't say anything about my occupation. We didn't want crosses burned in our backyard. What I do was not yet widely accepted by a lot of people. It is still not widely accepted today, but at least it is more prevalent thanks to the various television programs. Back then I did not work with clients on the phone or in remote locations., I set up appointments with my clients and they came to my house and we talked about their case in person.

I was married for twenty-six years, but my husband was not very present in the house, so for all practical purposes I was a single mom. I did anything I could to put food on the table. I've transported items to auction houses, I did woodwork as part of a craftsman's guild, and made lawn ornaments. I also operated a carpet cleaning business and was an auto detailer. At the same time I was working to support my family, I continued my psychic work, from readings to working on cases. I did not work as many cases while my kids were young as I do now, but I was still very busy and trying to help those who asked. Sometimes I found a family who put us up at their house, but that was only about 10 percent of the total. The other 90 percent came out of my own pocket. I can't help but feel the people's pain. I do something because I can.

Dustin finally graduated from high school. He had been playing music since he was ten. He composes all of his music on the computer, and he sings. He has a beautiful voice. He is still pursuing his music career. Diana is a nurse, Craig is working at a store, and Tamra works in the Home Health Care industry. Both Tamra and Diana take time to work on cases with me.

These days, they come over for holidays, and I drive over to their houses in Toledo, Ohio, but I live in Indiana.

Now I juggle my training classes, my readings with clients, and my paperwork for my training.

Today, for instance, in the midst of trying to get everything done—working on this book, on my training logs, and my clients—the phone rang and it was a retired state attorney who was working on a case. The police were saying the person's death was accidental and the family was alleging it was murder. I asked him to send me the information. He sent me the flood of pictures and so forth. So at this point, there went my schedule. I had to push things off until tomorrow.

And then I have to answer about seventeen phone calls, some cases, and some readings. Sometimes I am in training class with my dogs three weekends in a row. And then I have the kids pulling at me, with "This is happening in my life," or "I'm upset over this," plus my grandkids are always saying "Grandma, when are you coming?"

My grandkids are pretty much my world. I feel that because I don't get to see them as much I miss the changes they go through. Recently I went to see *Jersey Boys* with my youngest daughter, Tamra, and my granddaughter. We love musicals, and of course, being the teenager I am, I love Frankie Valli's music and so did my granddaughter. She's sixteen now. My grandson is nine. Those are the only two I have. Her name is Alexis, she is a typical sixteen year old, has a fantastic GPA, and I have no doubt she's going to go far. Brandon is very different from her, but very caring about other people's feelings, and he is very particular about things. I laugh and say he is a typical little Virgo.

I have had a boyfriend now for two and a half years. We met, and two weeks later we moved in together. This time I knew it was right, although I know there is no perfect relationship. There are deal breakers and not deal breakers. Just because they clang their spoon on their cup as they have tea, that's not a deal breaker. When you get older you realize there is nothing perfect. On Valentine's Day, 2012, he asked me to marry him. I told him he was crazy and I said, "If it ain't broke don't fix it." Then I looked at him and said, "You are serious aren't you?" He nodded. I laughed, and said, "Well, on that serious note I have to sleep on it." I could see the hurt look on his face.

The next morning after he left for work, I texted my answer to him. I said, "Yes, let's." I owed it to him because of the way he asked me. He did not do it in the conventional way at all, getting down on one knee. He just casually said, "You know, I figured out a way to get your knees fixed." (I had meniscal tears on both knees—and no health insurance.) "For us to get married." He said, "I wanted to ask you to marry me six months into our relationship, but I was afraid you would run." I said, "I would have run so fast it would have made your head spin!"

He is very supportive of my work—he has been the only person in my life who encourages me all the time. Sometimes when I go on my weekend training and I'm just exhausted, he says, "Listen you're just tired right now. This is what you want to do so just go do it." And he doesn't mind telling people at work he is with a psychic! He says, "I believe in you and I support you." That makes the juggling worthwhile.

He had his two dogs and I have my Border Collies and we acquired two cats. We have condo crates! Talk about a balancing act!

Chapter 27

WHY I DO IT

There is no such thing as closure. The pain always remains. I have felt and feel this pain as my own, which is why I do what I do. So much that after each case I have to sleep uninterruptedly for a week because I am so spent physically and emotionally.

I also do it because I have no other choice. The visions and impressions come to me and I have no means to stop them. When I first began to realize I had a mission, as it were, I simply surrendered to it and decided to refine my abilities instead of shutting them off. I would not have succeeded in that particular endeavor anyway.

Sometimes I do not succeed in either bringing home the missing or finding their remains. After those instances I want to pull my hair out. I wonder what was the stumbling block? What did I do or not do? Sometimes they simply do not want to be found. I first realized this was the case with Jimmy, although he eventually came around and I was able to find his body.

I have learned many lessons and received many gifts, especially from families of the missing. I don't judge or disbelieve anymore. I will question and learn before I shoot my big mouth off. Just because I don't understand something doesn't mean it isn't so. All things are possible. Just because we can't touch it, see it, or smell it, doesn't mean it's not there.

Sometimes things come to me and I don't always take them literally because they are more symbolic in nature. I may see a red car, but the car may not necessarily be red. The car is red because the person on the other side wanted to attract my attention to the car. I have to be careful what I say, because if I say that I saw a red car and later on I will see an entire screen of brown flash in front of me, I know it's a brown car, not red. Sometimes I see a black rose, which for me represents that the person has passed. These symbols aren't the same for every person. I have developed a language with them and am able to interpret what symbols I see into concrete messages, but it took a lot of time and trials to figure out what they meant. I was telling my student Travis that the messages he receives are individual to him. You have to use and understand your own language. Remember, we're not speaking English with them! We're drawing pictures in the sand. We're finding a way that we can comprehend them. It's not the same thing across the board. Sometimes I feel like I'm playing charades because sometimes characters like to play games, like Jimmy. It's also like playing a video game. Okay, I got to the cave, but I have to get the next clue in order to move on to the next level.

I think sometimes the skeptics, the ones who don't believe, refuse to believe because in some instances it is just too painful. My favorite type of skeptic is the chest-beater who says it's of the devil. I think the ones who say that the most are the ones who fear it the most. You can take sections of the Bible and make it fit whatever you want it to fit. That is where things get lost in translation. It's like playing the telephone game. You're supposed to repeat something the way you heard it, but by the time it gets to the fourth or fifth person it is nowhere near what it was.

"There is no way you can see anything because when you're dead, you're dead," the skeptics say. Then they turn around and say, "I have a feeling that's the way it is." I just start to laugh. Where did you get that feeling?

There are a lot of different ways the traumatic experience of remembering something you don't want to remember in which it is painful. Some people have been through certain situations, whether it be dreams or things they saw in past lives, that it becomes painful. As a child I had visions of past lives and I know it was me, but I just couldn't figure it out. I began piecing things together and tried to make sense of what I was seeing, hearing, and thinking. I remember laying down in an alley and looking up at the sky. A name suddenly popped into my head. I knew it was my name, but it was another name. Not Gale. I recently looked up the name on the Internet and discovered the name was of a person who really existed and had been shot.

My friends have heard me say I am my greatest skeptic. I have learned to question everything in different ways to see how it all really works. A lot of times when I said no, it's not so, I learned a lesson. I learned that I need to accept. I can question in a different way as far as understanding something, but I need to remain open-minded because all things are possible.

I have been accused many times of being emotionless. A television producer once said to me, "You are an emotionless bitch!" I replied, "Far better than being a drunken idiot." Spirits and spirit don't work together, and she sure swigged it down. I can cut to the quick, and I knew she completely understood my response.

I am not emotionless. Reporters understand that. I respect Larry King because of that. He never lost perspective during his years as a journalist, and I respect objectivity in a reporter more than anything. I have to maintain my focus and not point the finger. I cannot lose perspective because it will overshadow the impressions that I get. The more I can shut emotions down, the better. I have to focus on the pull and the draw as if I were a fish on a line, only I have to follow where the line leads me. I am not here to be the loony, lying psychic. I am here to tell people the truth. When you watch a psychic on television, they give you a fifteen-minute segment of a thirty-minute show and it looks like they solved the case in seconds. And I say, "Wait, I remember that case, it took months!" Television just isn't real life.

Chapter 28

THE FUTURE

I never really call a case closed. I can't say that I see into the future, but I do know when the timing is right for some of these people to come home. It might not be me who brings them home, but does it matter if it's me or not? The only thing that matters is they come home.

I feel that we are closer on Grace's case, the young Indiana University student. Each time, I feel like I get a little closer. Unfortunately I don't have months to spend there, so I have to take it in short spurts. I am definitely going back. I left with a feeling that there are some areas I need to cover but I am going to need some help. Gary (the crime-scene investigator) and I have spoken about this and we are gathering information on what we need to go back on that case. It is hard to describe the feeling, but I get a sense that I am are really close to something; that something is coming to a head. I did name the days they would find Jimmy and in the Japan case. I'm not close enough yet here to name a date for Grace, but it's coming. It kind of gnaws at me.

Ben, the handsome second-year medical student, will forever be in my heart. I cannot tell the many times I have shed tears over it because of how close Barry and I got, as parents. I want to keep my promise to Barry that I will bring Ben home. I also need extra help, in terms of searchers, in this case in Columbus, Ohio. I wouldn't doubt it if the folks from Texas came over to help us.

I will continue to work the case about the missing woman in Illinois with Jim, the private investigator, and will go back as long and as often as money allows it. We have very specific areas we are checking on that case. Every part of a search represents money so it takes time, which is why these cases are not solved in fifteen minutes like on television. Sometimes it's timing and sometimes lack of funds. But I will never give up.

I would like to go back and search for Abdul because I feel that I just got lip service from law enforcement. According to the people in the village, nobody went back to search after we went there. I realize some areas don't have the funds to do it and the area where he went missing is a dangerous area. I would like to get the funds and go back. That was almost like the Florida case, when I felt I was in the correct area when I went on the blind drive for the missing girl. If I drive an area and a person is there, I will know it. There is no mistaking that feeling. It's like being punched in the stomach. But I have to get past those feelings and continue to work. I will continue to work on cases as long as people continue to kill each other.

"For those who believe, no proof is necessary.
For those who don't believe, no proof is possible."

—STUART CHASE

To Write to the Authors

If you wish to contact the author or would like more information about this book, please write to the author in care of Llewellyn Worldwide Ltd. and we will forward your request. Both the author and publisher appreciate hearing from you and learning of your enjoyment of this book and how it has helped you. Llewellyn Worldwide Ltd. cannot guarantee that every letter written to the author can be answered, but all will be forwarded. Please write to:

Gale St. John and Diana Montane
⁒ Llewellyn Worldwide
2143 Wooddale Drive
Woodbury, MN 55125-2989

Please enclose a self-addressed stamped envelope for reply, or $1.00 to cover costs. If outside the U.S.A., enclose an international postal reply coupon.

GET MORE AT LLEWELLYN.COM

Visit us online to browse hundreds of our books and decks, plus sign up to receive our e-newsletters and exclusive online offers.

- **• Free tarot readings • Spell-a-Day • Moon phases**
- **• Recipes, spells, and tips • Blogs • Encyclopedia**
- **• Author interviews, articles, and upcoming events**

GET SOCIAL WITH LLEWELLYN

www.Facebook.com/LlewellynBooks

Follow us on

www.Twitter.com/Llewellynbooks

GET BOOKS AT LLEWELLYN

LLEWELLYN ORDERING INFORMATION

Order online: Visit our website at www.llewellyn.com to select your books and place an order on our secure server.

Order by phone:
- Call toll free within the U.S. at 1-877-NEW-WRLD (1-877-639-9753)
- Call toll free within Canada at 1-866-NEW-WRLD (1-866-639-9753)
- We accept VISA, MasterCard, and American Express

Order by mail:
Send the full price of your order (MN residents add 6.875% sales tax) in U.S. funds, plus postage and handling to: Llewellyn Worldwide, 2143 Wooddale Drive Woodbury, MN 55125-2989

POSTAGE AND HANDLING

STANDARD (U.S. & Canada):
(Please allow 12 business days)
$25.00 and under, add $4.00.
$25.01 and over, FREE SHIPPING.

INTERNATIONAL ORDERS (airmail only):
$16.00 for one book, plus $3.00 for each additional book.

Visit us online for more shipping options. Prices subject to change.

FREE CATALOG!

To order, call
1-877-
NEW-WRLD
ext. 8236
or visit our
website

FORGOTTEN BURIAL

A CRY FOR JUSTICE FROM BEYOND THE GRAVE

JODI FOSTER

Forgotten Burial
A Cry for Justice from Beyond the Grave
JODI FOSTER

When Jodi Foster returned to her California hometown with her young daughter, she never could have imagined the terror and confusion she experienced in the nights that followed. On top of her terrifyingly real nightmares of abduction and murder, Jodi witnessed lights flashing on and off, clocks going haywire, and her daughter's doll repeatedly screaming, "I feel great!"

Forgotten Burial tells Jodi's true paranormal story unraveling the mystery behind the unsolved case of a missing young woman, Madeline Isabella Johnson. After moving into Madeline's last known residence, Jodi and her daughter reveal clues about what happened to the disappeared girl through ghostly encounters, vivid dreams, and divine intervention. Join Jodi on her reality-bending adventure as she works with police to bring justice to this disturbing, yet ultimately uplifting story.

978-0-7387-3926-7, 288 pp., 5³/₁₆ x 8   **$15.99**

The True Ghost Story of a
Reluctant Psychic

A Haunted Life

Debra Robinson

A Haunted Life
The True Ghost Story of a Reluctant Psychic
Debra Robinson

Debra Robinson faced haunted houses, terrifying psychic encounters, shattered dreams, and a battle with evil. But nothing prepared her for the death of the two most important people in her life.

Born psychic and raised in a religious family, Debra Robinson felt conflicted all her life about using her gifts. And when, at an early age, she attracts something evil with a Ouija board, she embarks on a lengthy battle with darkness. With her career as a professional musician taking her on the road, she experiences brushes with fame and heartbreak that serve to strengthen her resolve. Struggling to come to terms with her psychic gifts, the tragic deaths of her only child and her beloved father—and their visits from the other side—finally leave her with a sense of understanding and the strength to love herself.

978-0-7387-3641-9, 288 pp., 5³/₁₆ x 8   **$16.99**

Miraculous Moments
for the Bereaved

our children
live on

ELISSA AL-CHOKHACHY

Our Children Live On
Miraculous Moments for the Bereaved
Elissa Al-Chokhachy

Our Children Live On is an uplifting collection of powerful, true stories that prove our children are with us forever. These heartfelt, moving testimonials—from parents, grandparents, siblings, friends, and caregivers—demonstrate that love and life are truly eternal.

Anyone who has suffered the unimaginable loss of a loved one—especially a child—will find hope and comfort in these miraculous stories. There are incredibly vivid dreams and visits, transcendent moments of an invisible hug or a familiar voice, and unmistakable signs of a child's undying love. Also featured are extraordinary accounts of near-death experiences and the visions that often occur to those near death.

978-0-7387-3135-3, 336 pp., 6 x 9   **$16.99**